Anonymous

Beginner's guide to photography:

Showing how to buy a camera and how to use it including practical remarks upon

photographic apparatus generally, how to take a photograph, development,

printing from the negative, taking instantaneous pictures

Anonymous

Beginner's guide to photography:
Showing how to buy a camera and how to use it including practical remarks upon photographic apparatus generally, how to take a photograph, development, printing from the negative, taking instantaneous pictures

ISBN/EAN: 9783337775148

Printed in Europe, USA, Canada, Australia, Japan

Cover: Foto ©ninafisch / pixelio.de

More available books at **www.hansebooks.com**

Fourth Edition, Revised and Enlarged.
32nd Thousand.

BEGINNER'S GUIDE
TO
PHOTOGRAPHY.

Copyright.

PRESS OPINIONS.

Third Edition. Beginner's Guide to Photography

LAND AND WATER.
"The Beginner's Guide to Photography. Anyone who had never taken a [photograph?] in his life could go to work with confidence with this guide by his side."

INVENTION.
"'Beginner's Guide to Photography.' (Messrs. Perken, Son and Rayment, Hatton Garden, E.C.) This is a very practical guide, in which useful advice is given [how to] buy a camera, and how to use it. Any beginner would be able to learn from the [direc]tions given how to take a photograph."

CHRISTIAN.
"'Beginner's Guide to Photography.' (6d. Perken, Son and Rayment, 99 [Hatton] Garden.) This is a valuable and cheap little book, which all tyro-amateur photo[graphers] would do well to peruse carefully before investing in apparatus, as they may [save] considerable expense."

ENGINEER.
"'Beginner's Guide to Photography,' showing how to buy a camera and how [to use] it. (Messrs. Perken, Son and Rayment.) This is a useful little book, probably the [cheapest] published, but at the same time satisfactory as a concise guide to amateurs. [It gives] practical hints on apparatus, and clear explanations of the methods of taking and [developing] photographs, on enlarging and on reducing, on the producing of lantern s[lides, with] instructions on the materials required. It is illustrated, and may be recommend[ed to the] beginner."

PHOTOGRAPHY.
"'The Beginner's Guide to Photography,' Perken, Son and Rayment, 99, [Hatton] Garden, London, E.C. This little manual is one of the most clearly written b[rief] books in the market. If any of our tyro readers want to pick up a few wrinkles [they will] find a wonderfully lucid instructor in the 'Beginner's Guide.'"

BUILDING NEWS.
"Architects desirous of becoming their own photographers will do well to inv[est in this] sixpenny 'Beginner's Guide to Photography,' published by Messrs. Perken, S[on and] Rayment, of 99, Hatton Garden. It is the most complete and practical cheap ha[ndbook on] the art we have seen."

CITIZEN.
"'The Beginner's Guide to Photography,' (6d.; Perken, Son and Rayment, [99, Hatton] Garden) is a remarkably useful little volume which gives to the amateur photogra[pher clear] and concise directions. without those confusing technicalities which characterise mo[st works] of a similar nature."

THE MORNING NEWS.
"'Beginner's Guide to Photography.'—This work has been favourably menti[oned by] those organs of the English Press most capable of forming an opinion of its merits. [He who] reads may photograph. The publishers are Perken, Son and Rayment, of 99, [Hatton] Garden, London."

THE ACADEMY.
"'Beginner's Guide to Photography,' (Perken, Son and Rayment.) There a[re no] more expensive books published on photography that do not contain half the real [useful] advice that is to be found in the hundred pages of this little guide. It can be sa[fely relied] upon by the novice, and covers his requirements from his first purchase of an outfit t[ill he is] far advanced in the art."

SPORTSMAN.
"'The Beginner's Guide to Photography' (Perken, Son and Rayment, 99, [Hatton] Garden, E.C.) is one of the best and most comprehensive works of instruction to t[he art] of manipulating photographic apparatus that we remember to have come across."

SPORTING TIMES.
"One of the best 'Guides to Photography' is Perken, Son and Rayment's, pu[blished] at sixpence. It really is cheap. You have a description of apparatus, a description of [taking] a photograph, development, printing from the negative, expenditure, and goodness [knows] what. Send to 99, Hatton Garden, you photographic beginners. Don't forget the sta[mps.]"

PRESS OPINIONS.

Third Edition.   *Beginner's Guide to Photography,*   **6d·**

GRAPHIC.
"The 'Beginner's Guide to Photography' (Perken, Son and Rayment), by a 'Fellow of the Chemical Society,' is a useful little manual for amateur photographers. It contains brief and concise directions for taking, developing, and printing the negative, while there is a valuable article on that bugbear of all amateurs—'Exposure,' by Mr. A. S Platts, containing some exceedingly useful exposure tables."

DAILY NEWS.
"Under the title of the 'Beginner's Guide to Photography,' by a 'Fellow of the Chemical Society,' Perken, Son and Rayment have published a useful handbook for all interested in the art of photography. An article on 'Exposure,' and some carefully compiled exposure tables, by Mr. A. S. Platts, must be of value to all amateurs."

St. STEPHEN'S REVIEW.
"'Beginner's Guide to Photography,' published by Perken, Son and Rayment, 99, Hatton Garden, London.—The fashionable art science, Photography, is most explicitly set forth without the confusing technicalities employed in most works on this subject. The difficult matter of 'Choice of Apparatus' has a chapter devoted to it, in which the special advantages of each kind of camera and lens is detailed. Altogether this book may be said to be of the greatest value to all who practise photography."

ILLUSTRATED SPORTING & DRAMATIC.
"The 'Beginner's Guide to Photography.'—With this title a six penny book has been published by Messrs. Perken, Son and Rayment, of 99, Hatton Garden, which we find both simple and practical. By following its instructions carefully the amateur will save much disappointment in the sense of blurred pictures, and much expense for spoilt plates."

MORNING POST.
"The 'Beginner's Guide to Photography' is one of the best works on this popular and fascinating art yet published. The author thoroughly understands his subject. Messrs. Perken, Son and Rayment, Hatton Garden, are the publishers."

WHITEHALL REVIEW.
"'Beginner's Guide to Photography.' (Perken, Son and Rayment.)—This is an excellent treatise which all amateurs who have taken up photography as an amusement should peruse."

ARMY & NAVY GAZETTE,
"Messrs. Perken, Son and Rayment send us the second edition of their 'Beginner's Guide to Photography,' a plain and practical handbook as to how to buy and use a camera, with many particulars concerning lenses and other matters, for which the publishers are celebrated as makers."

COURT JOURNAL.
"Messrs. Perken, Son and Rayment, one of the largest and most popular makers of photographic apparatus, publish a most useful little work entitled, 'Beginner's Guide to Photography,' in which the several operations of taking, developing and printing the photograph are described with great clearness, and in a manner suitable to those who are handling a camera for the first time. While those who have not yet provided themselves with the necessary apparatus cannot do better than peruse the valuable chapter on 'The Choice of Apparatus,' and patronise this firm for their purchases."

JEWELLER & METALWORKER.
"'Beginner's Guide,' published by Messrs. Perken, Son and Rayment, of 99, Hatton Garden, at the small sum of six pence. It is a work which can be relied upon, and the language of it is easy of comprehension, a great merit in works of this description."

ILLUSTRATED LONDON NEWS.
'The 'Beginner's Guide to Photography,' published by Messrs. Perken, Son and Rayment, of Hatton Garden, treats clearly and concisely of the apparatus and requirements necessary to engage in the delightful pastime of photography, and will be found most useful to amateurs."

LADY'S PICTORIAL.
"'Beginner's Guide to Photography.' (Perken, Son and Rayment, 'Optimus.') Revised and enlarged edition, 6d. It is clear and explicit, quite free from unnecessary and confusing technicalities. I can safely recommend this little work to any of our readers who contemplate taking up photography."

ENGLISH MECHANIC.
"'Beginner's Guide to Photography.' Messrs. Perken, Son and Rayment, of Hatton Garden, have issued a second edition of this useful little work, which has already reached a very large sale."

TO
PHOTOGRAPHY;

SHOWING

HOW TO BUY A CAMERA

AND HOW TO USE IT.

INCLUDING PRACTICAL REMARKS UPON

PHOTOGRAPHIC APPARATUS GENERALLY—HOW TO TAKE A PHOTOGRAPH—DEVELOPMENT—PRINTING FROM THE NEGATIVE—TAKING INSTANTANEOUS PICTURES—PRODUCING LANTERN SLIDES—PHOTO· MICROGRAPHY AND ENLARGING.

BY

A FELLOW OF THE CHEMICAL SOCIETY.

PUBLISHED BY

PERKEN, SON & RAYMENT,

99, HATTON GARDEN, LONDON, E.C.

CHOICE OF APPARATUS.

THE photographic aspirant will probably find very great difficulty in choosing suitable apparatus with which to make a commencement. He will see by various advertisements that apparatus can be purchased at greatly differing prices. Passing by those makers who profess to supply everything necessary for two or three shillings —and at once relegating them and their wares to the toy-shop—we next come to complete sets sold at two or three guineas. For about this sum a complete set of apparatus can be had of the type shown at page 114. The items include a camera and its belongings, the necessary chemicals, a red lamp, a dozen gelatine plates, and many other requisites. It is the kind of set which would be very suitable to place in the hands of an intelligent youth—and moreover, it will produce good pictures if landscapes—pure and simple—be the only ones attempted. It is furnished with a cheap form of lens which is only suitable for this class of work; but it is a lens which will do this work as efficiently as others which are far more expensive. But it is only right to mention that the higher priced lens will do for other more advanced pictures as well. This form of "single lens," as it is called, is described in the Chapter upon lenses.

He who wishes to excel in the Art of Photography must furnish himself with apparatus of a somewhat more advanced type, and—as in many other pursuits— his wants must be regulated by the length of his purse. For a ten-pound note, or thereabouts, he can obtain a camera, lens, and stand, which will produce for him pictures which he will not be ashamed to show to his friends. If his means are limited, he will do best to commence with a small camera. That size known as half-plate is a very good one for a beginner. There is not a very great difference in the price of this sized camera, and the one next size larger to it, for the workmanship in both is of much the same value. The inexperienced buyer may, therefore, be tempted to pay the higher sum to secure the larger camera. But he must remember that the larger sized camera entails larger sized gelatine plates, larger quantities of chemicals, and larger everything else. Indeed he is in the position of a man who has the choice of buying a large and a small house, without there being very much difference in the purchase money of either. If a wise man, he will first count the cost of keeping up the larger house before he decides upon having it. We will now append a list of the various sizes of photographic cameras, each size given denoting the size of the picture which the camera will give. We also state against each size the price per dozen of the gelatine plates upon which the pictures are taken :—

Camera giving pictures of the undermentioned size in inches.		Cost of gelatine plates.	
$4\frac{1}{4} \times 3\frac{1}{4}$	generally known as quarter-plate size	from 1/- to	1/9 per doz.
5×4	... ...	,, 1/7 ,,	3/- ,,
$6\frac{3}{4} \times 3\frac{1}{4}$	Stereoscopic size ...	,, 2/2 ,,	4/6 ,,
$6\frac{1}{2} \times 4\frac{3}{4}$	Half plate size ...	,, 2/3 ,,	4/6 ,,
$7\frac{1}{4} \times 4\frac{1}{2}$	... ...	,, 2/10 ,,	5/6 ,,
$7\frac{1}{2} \times 5$	... ...	,, 3/5 ,,	6/- ,,
8×5	... ...	,, 3/10 ,,	7/- ,,
$8\frac{1}{2} \times 6\frac{1}{2}$	Whole plate ...	,, 4/3 ,,	7/6 ,,
9×7	... ...	,, 5/- ,,	10/- ,,
10×8	... ...	,, 7/3 ,,	12/6 ,,
12×10	... ...	,, 10/6 ,,	16/- ,,
15×12	... ...	,, 18/- ,,	28/- ,,

Those who are fortunate in being so placed that they

have no need to study economy in such a matter, cannot do better than purchase a camera of a good medium size—such as $8\frac{1}{2} \times 6\frac{1}{2}$, or 10×8. Or perhaps the wiser plan would be to commence with a smaller size, and adopt the larger one later on. There is another alternative. A large camera can be bought in the first instance, and the dark slides, or double backs for holding the plates, can be fitted by the vendor with carriers to hold small-sized gelatine plates. The operator can then use these small plates until proficient, and can afterwards relinquish the carriers, and use plates the full size of the apparatus. Adopting this plan, his experimental pictures —with their faulty results—will not cost him very much.

There are one or two points which should be looked for in a good camera. In the first place it should be rigid when set up on its stand, so that it will not vibrate with every breeze. In the next place, its parts should be so arranged that it will not only pack up into a small compass for travelling, but that it will readily unpack. Some makers sacrifice everything to extreme lightness; their cameras are wonders of mechanical skill, but are generally wanting in rigidity, are easily broken, and have too many complications.

A capital form of camera is that shown at page 111. The first picture is a front view of the instrument, with its board as yet unpierced for the lens. It will be seen that the front of the instrument can be moved up and down, or from right to left. It has a leather bellows body—an indispensable feature of all first class cameras—of such a length that long focus lenses can be employed as well as those of short focus. This is a most important point, the value of which will soon become evident to the operator. The focussing, or lengthening and shortening of this bellows body is brought about by the side screw knob shown at the bottom of the figure which works a pinion over a rack, giving an exact adjustment,

Referring now to the back elevation (page 111), we notice that the back can be swung in any direction. The instrument possesses not only the usual swing back, as it is called, but has a side swing as well. At the top of the back will be noticed two screw knobs with milled heads. These knobs are at the ends of rods which pass right through the framework of the camera to the base board below. By loosening these the back can be placed at any required angle, and by tightening them that angle is rigidly preserved as long as may be necessary.

A still more compact camera is shewn at page 110. This form possesses all the advantages of that just described, but its movements are simplified in such a manner that it can be unfolded, and made ready for taking a picture in the space of a very few seconds. This camera is of square section, but is made to take the usual standard sizes of plates. The object of making it square, is that the back may be reversed if necessary. In the older forms of cameras, if it were desired to take a picture on the long diameter of the plate, as in the case of a full length portrait for instance, it was necessary to unscrew the camera from its stand, and screw it up again so that it rested on its side. A screw hole was always provided for this purpose. The operation not only consumed some time, but it was awkward in the extreme, to use the instrument in an unaccustomed position. In the camera under discussion this is obviated by making the back reversible, and it can be reversed in about 4 seconds. We can thus obtain horizontal, or vertical pictures at will, and change and change about with the greatest celerity, while the camera remains fixed to the tripod stand. This camera illustrates a new adjunct which must not pass unnoticed. It shows a patent focussing screen that can be fitted to any camera, which will slide in and out, so that it can be adjusted to the focussing position of any dark slide, roll-holder, or other contrivance which may be invented for taking negatives on paper, and other material. There are at present several roller slides or holders in the market which are used for producing pictures—panorama fashion—on long bands of paper. These contrivances are at present on their trial, and it is impossible to say whether they will or will not partly supersede the use of glass for photographic work. Should they prove to be as successful as their promoters believe they will, the purchaser of one of these cameras with its adjustable focussing screen, can march with the times without relinquishing his old apparatus. Any roll holder can be readily fitted to a camera with this adjunct. This camera may be folded up into a marvellously small compass for travelling.

In page 111 is shown a camera of another description, known as The Universal, which is intended for portraiture in the studio, or sitting room. Now, thanks to dry plates, most excellent portraits can be, and are constantly taken in private rooms. The camera in question is of a more solid description than those previously described, and has a fixed base. The focussing screw is placed at the back immediately underneath the ground glass screen, and the camera has a repeating back, an arrangement by which two portraits in different positions can be taken upon one plate.

The camera depicted at page 126 does not call for any special remark, but it illustrates two accessories which are worthy of mention, and which are used for taking instantaneous pictures. The one is a "view finder" placed on the top of the instrument, and the other is an instantaneous shutter, to be presently more fully described, which covers the lens aperture. These valuable additions can be fitted to any form of camera. The object of the view finder is to give a reduced image of the same picture which falls upon the sensitive plate directly exposure is made. In taking a picture of a moving object, such as a ship in full sail, it is all important that that object should fall in its right place in the composition, so that an harmonious picture may result. The operator can secure this end by watching the image in the view finder. Directly the moving object gets into the best position with regard to the other elements of the picture, the instantaneous shutter is released, and in the twinkling of an eye the picture is taken. The other cameras figured do not require any description, but we may notice a useful type of quarter plate instrument, with its three double backs and leather case, page 112, which is peculiarly fitted for the tourist, who does not require large pictures. A still smaller instrument is made for those interested in the Magic Lantern, its double dark slides carry plates $3\frac{1}{4}$ square, the usual size for lantern slides. The weight bulk of this camera is quite inconsiderable.

A camera which is rigid and firm in all its parts is of little avail unless it be mounted on a stand having the same qualities. Figs. on page 119 show different forms of stands in which these characteristics are carefully preserved. In this page the stand is shown extended ready for the reception of the camera, and is also shown closed and strapped up for transport. The way in which the legs fold up is also well shown; and it may be observed that each leg can be readily shortened at will without shifting the camera. This is an important advantage, especially when the operator is obliged to place his apparatus on uneven ground. The rigidity of these tripod stands is ensured in setting them up for use by utilizing the natural elasticity of the wood. In spite of their light weight—the smaller sizes weighing less than 3 lbs., a weight of 56 lbs. can be suspended from the centre of the triangular top without causing any undue strain upon the various parts. The camera is in all cases attached to the stand by a brass thumb-screw, which is supplied with the apparatus.

An ingenious improvement in portable stands has recently been devised. It is styled "Rayment's Patent" tripod top (see page 126). This, instead of being made in one piece as such tops usually are, is in two pieces, one above the other. In the lower portion a sliding board runs, which is hinged to the upper half; this enables the camera to be turned instantaneously on its side for the purpose of taking upright pictures. By using the sliding piece already described, the camera is brought central over the legs of the tripod, the structure remaining perfectly rigid. Another advantage gained by this contrivance is, that by turning the camera when fixed by the T screw to the tripod top, so that the lens points upwards, photographs may be readily secured of the beautiful ceilings to be found in many of our ancient and modern buildings, thus meeting a want often experienced.

Again, should a drawing, map. or other such design require to be copied, it can be easily accomplished by reversing the position just described and pointing the lens downwards towards the floor, where the object is spread out between the legs of the tripod.

Before describing the various operations involved in producing a photographic picture, we may call attention to one more very necessary piece of apparatus, namely, the red lamp. It is a fortunate thing for photography that the chemicals employed, although so sensitive to white light that a picture can be obtained in the smallest fraction of a second of time, are insensitive, or nearly so, to red rays of light. Were it otherwise, photography would be almost an impossibility—unless men were gifted with the power of seeing in darkness. As it is, the operator conducts all his work—except the business of actually taking the picture—by red light. The professional has, of course, his dark room, in which the daylight is filtered through some kind of ruby medium. But to carry on .work at night—or away from home, when plates have to be changed, and even developed in out-of-the-way cupboards or cellars—a red lamp is a *sine quâ non*. The form of lamp shown at page 121 presents a great many advantages. It possesses a powerful paraffin lamp, so arranged that the oil receptacle is isolated from the flame, and cannot get heated. It has a sliding door at the back, so constructed with guarded loopholes that plenty of air can get in and out, but no ray of white light can steal outside. In front are two large panes of ruby glass.

A less expensive form of lamp is made (this is the lamp shown in the set at page 121), in which two sides of the lamp are of metal, and the third of red glass. The metal sides are hinged together so that they will fold up for travelling, with the ruby glass protected from fracture by lying between them. Top and bottom triangular pieces—one forming a candle holder, and the other a chimney—complete this clever little arrangement.

We may in this connection also notice a portable tent which has been very lately introduced, and which may rightly be regarded as the latest novelty in the world of photography. It is shaped like an umbrella, and is known as the "Patent Eclipse Ruby Tent." Like an umbrella, it folds up in very small space, 30 × 3 inches, and can be set up for plate changing or developing purposes as easily as its well-known prototype. It is shown at page 115. Made of two thicknesses of material, canary color under ruby or black, no light can enter it except through its window of ruby fabric. It is unnecessary to use a ruby lamp. Daylight, or the light from an ordinary lamp or candle placed outside the tent, shining through the ruby and canary materials of which it is made amply illuminates the interior. The head and hands are introduced so that the operator, either at home or abroad, sitting in a chair, can conveniently watch the progress of his work whilst the tent rests on the table. For the summer tourist such a tent is indispensable ; but for general use it represents a distinct gain to the photographer, being very preferable to the stuffy cupboards often employed as makeshifts for dark rooms by beginners.

PHOTOGRAPHIC LENSES.

THE most simple form of camera lens, is that known as the single view lens. In reality it does not consist of a single piece of glass, but of two, sometimes three cemented together, so as to appear, when examined, to be one glass. It is a most valuable lens when used for landscape (see page 109), but owing to the defect which it has of slightly distorting any straight lines near the margin of the picture, it cannot be used—except with certain precautions—for architectural subjects. It is supplied with the cheaper sets of apparatus, and will afford very fine pictures, if kept to its own particular class of work.

A more expensive lens, and the form used more commonly than any other, is the rectilinear (see page 108), which, as its name tells us, gives lines free from distortion. This lens might be termed the sheet anchor of the photographer. It will do for landscape, for architecture, for portraiture, for copying, and for enlarging. It is also the best lens to employ for instantaneous pictures. It consists of two achromatic lenses of precisely similar pattern, placed in a tube with their concave surfaces facing one another. Between them is a slit for the insertion of stops or diaphragms of varying size. A great advantage in the use of this form of lens is, that one lens can be removed and the other employed as a single lens, under which circumstances it gives an image double the size of that afforded by the complete arrangement. At the same time the camera must be opened out to double its former length. In choosing a camera, therefore, this power of extension should not be lost sight of.

In the wide angle doublet, or portable symmetrical lens (see page 108), we also have a combination of two lenses. This form of lens is especially valuable for taking subjects in confined situations, for it will include in the picture it gives, a great deal more than would a lens of longer focus. It is for this reason well adapted for pourtraying interiors of buildings, where the camera must be placed in comparative close proximity to the subject to be taken. It is also valuable for copying.

The portrait lens (page 109), is the most rapid of all lenses, for it was devised at a time when the chemical part of the art was backward, and when every effort had to be made on the part of the optician to lessen the time of exposure. It takes excellent portraits with the rapid plates now in the market, it can be used for copying, enlarging, or as an objective for the lantern. It is, therefore, a useful tool in the hands of an intelligent worker. At the same time it will not do for landscape photography. He who is limited to the purchase of one lens, should get one of the rectilinear form. He can afterwards add to his stock as opportunity offers, with the certainty that every additional lens will give him increasing power over King Sol. We may call special attention to a make of lenses stamped with the word "Optimus." As that name implies, they are among the best in the market.

A lens is now constructed (page 107) the rapidity of which nearly approaches that of the Portrait Lens, whilst for definition and depth of focus it is superior. This instrument is known as the "Euryscope" and possesses a working aperture of F 6. It is well suited for both portraits and landscape photographs, and for copying and enlarging is unsurpassed.

A wide-angle form of Euroscope working at F9.50 is also to be obtained (page 107). It is a most difficult lens to make, but is scarcely to be equalled for general utility.

TAKING A PHOTOGRAPH.

THE operations involved in taking a photograph may be roughly grouped under two heads. Firstly, the optical part of the business, and secondly, the chemical part. Luckily these two divisions can now be kept quite separate and distinct from one another, so that the amount of impedimenta which the operator takes into the field with him, where the first part of the process is executed, is but a small portion of the necessaries required in taking a photograph. Things were indeed different in the old days of wet collodion plates. The traveller had then to carry all his stock of chemicals with him, for unless the chemical part of the process followed immediately upon the exposure of the sensitive plate in the camera, that plate would be inevitably spoilt. Now, thanks to dry plates, the travelling photographer is quite independent of his bottles, chemicals, and dishes. These are left at home until opportunity occurs when he can introduce them to the plates which he has exposed in his camera during his walks abroad.

The interval which occurs between the two operations of exposure and development may be a few hours, or may be extended to weeks or months. The writer has often during a photographic tour extending over many weeks, left the development of his plates until long after returning to his home, and has seldom found his pictures to suffer by being left uncared for so long. But he by no means recommends this practice, for a slight accident may spoil a negative, and the mischief is not found out until the owner is so far away that another negative taken at the same spot is quite out of the question. Let him cite a case in point. He was staying not long ago on the South Coast, some few miles from Dover. He paid a visit to this town chiefly for the purpose of taking various parts of the old castle, and pictures of certain evidences of the Roman occupation of Britain, which abound in the place. From one particular point he obtained a splendid view of the old fortress, and was fortunate in having a lens with him, which just included on his focussing screen the entire view. He took this picture, and followed it by one of the old Pharos which crowns the hill upon which Dover Castle stands. He attached quite as much importance to the one picture as to the other. Luckily he happened to develope his plates on this occasion while still in the neighbourhood, and found to his intense disgust, that Dover Castle was hopelessly jumbled up with the old Roman light-house. He had taken both views on one plate. The accident was soon remedied at the cost of another day's work, and a climb with the apparatus up to the top of the Castle hill. Such a mishap as this can be easily avoided by a simple precaution. The photographer should carry with him a few strips of gummed paper, which he can get for the asking at any post-office. When a plate has been exposed, gum a piece of this paper across the corner of the shutter which covers it, so that that shutter cannot again be withdrawn without breaking the paper. A memorandum of the subject can also be scribbled with a pencil across the gummed slip. With these few words of caution respecting a difficulty into which it is very easy to fall, we will now enumerate as briefly as possible the necessary precautions to observe in taking a picture.

Let the first attempt be made of a view from a window, if it be only chimney pots. Set the camera up on its stand, uncover the lens and focus the picture as sharply as possible on the ground glass screen provided for the purpose. The focussing cloth is thrown over the head during the operation, and should well cover the camera as well. It is not a bad plan to have attached to the focussing cloth a little elastic loop, which will go over the lens in front. After the view is focussed, put in one of the stops or diaphragms provided with the lens, and notice how the aspect of the picture on the ground glass is modified. It is not so bright as it was, but the details are much sharper than they were before. Use, say, the smallest stop but one; and until experience teaches more familiarity with the camera and its belongings, use no other.

When the view is focussed to satisfaction, cap the lens, throw the ground glass screen out of its place, and retire to the dark room. Here, by the dim light of the red lamp, take a couple of plates out of their containing box, and put them in one of the double backs, taking care that as the back lies open like a book in front of you, that the film, or dull side of the plates is placed downwards. Avoid touching the surface of the plates with the fingers; but brush them over with a flat camel's hair brush kept for the purpose, before inserting the plates in the double back. Close up the plate box, as well as the double slide, and take the latter to the camera. Insert the double back in the groove provided for it, cover the camera with the focussing cloth, and placing your hand underneath, carefully draw the shutter of the slide. Your gelatine plate is now ready for exposure, and when the cap of the lens is removed the light will act upon it. Remove the cap for, say, three seconds, and immediately replace it. You may now reverse the double back, and take another picture, this time letting it have five seconds' exposure. When the two plates are afterwards developed and finished, it will be seen which negative has the brighter appearance, and the power of the lens, as well as the rapidity of the plates employed, can be judged accordingly. One more word about exposure. Get a note-book, and note at first, the details of every exposure made; such as time of day, time of year, state of the weather, and so on. By studying this book, side by side with the negatives to which it refers, a great deal may be learnt. Correct exposure is the most important part of the business of photography, and is a thing which can only be learnt by constant practice and attention to details.

It is quite impossible to write down anything definite with regard to the length of time for which the lens must be uncovered. If we had only one particular subject to photograph, and this subject were always lighted by the same amount of daylight, it would be an easy matter to calculate the amount of exposure required with every diaphragm of a lens, provided that the necessary amount had been ascertained by experiment with but one of those diaphragms. For these stops or diaphragms, as furnished with modern lenses, have apertures bearing a definite relation to one another. As a general rule each diaphragm will require double the exposure needed for the next size larger. Or to put it in another way—suppose the smallest stop of a lens to require an exposure of 24 seconds with a given subject, with the next size larger the exposure will be 12, then 6, then 3, then 1½, until we come to the full aperture of the lens, by which the picture can be taken in ¾ of a second. But as a matter of fact, the exposure varies not only with the nature of the subject, but with the time of day, the time of year, and the state of the atmosphere. The old adage, "*Experientia docet*," cannot be more aptly quoted than in connection with this question of exposure.

As a rough guide to the worker a table is appended by which he may learn the very great difference there is in the exposure required for different subjects. Let us suppose that he is working with a gelatine plate of average sensitiveness, and is using a medium sized stop. For the reasons given above, such a table can only be regarded as a hint to workers—not as an infallible guide. It must be read in conjunction with what has been already said with regard to time of day, state or atmosphere, etc.

The medium stop of a rectilinear lens will require the varying exposures noted below :—

$\frac{1}{80}$ sec.	Sky and Sea.
$\frac{1}{2}$ sec.	Open Fields.
1 to 2 secs.	Landscape with trees close at hand.
3 secs. up to 3 or more minutes.	Under trees, in woods and forests.
10 minutes.	Interior of rooms, well lighted.
$\frac{1}{2}$-an-hour to 2 hours.	Interiors badly lighted, or artificially lighted.

In making out this short table, the writer—who has worked for years with one description of lens, and one description of dry plate—has relied solely upon observations noted in his own practice. In the next Chapter we show how the exposed plates can be developed.

DEVELOPMENT.

A Photographic beginner will be apt to imagine that if a plate has been exposed in the camera, that it will at once bear an image of the subject upon which it has been exposed, and he will probably be surprised when he is told that the plate bears exactly the same appearance after that operation which it did before. But all the same, a change has taken place, and an important change too, but as yet it is invisible. The plate now bears, what is commonly called, a latent image, but this image only becomes visible under the operation, called development.

There are several different methods by which a gelatine plate can be developed, but it is a safe rule to adopt the formula recommended by the makers of the particular plates used. It is the invariable custom for makers of plates to issue with them plain directions for their development, but as these instructions are necessarily brief, we will endeavour to explain in detail the various operations necessary. We will also give one or two different formulæ which will be found to produce good negatives with most of the plates now sold.

First of all we will describe the method most commonly in vogue in this country, and which is known as alkaline development. The chemicals required are the following, which should be purchased of some reliable dealer in photographic requisites:—

  Pyrogallic Acid,
  Liquor Ammonia (880),
  Bromide of Potassium,
  Alum,
  Hyposulphite of Soda.

It will be of some assistance to the beginner if we make one or two remarks with reference to these chemicals. Pyrogallic acid is a snow-white woolly powder, so light that a one ounce bottle of it would contain about twelve ounces of water. One ounce, costing about sixteen pence, is sufficient for developing many dozens of small pictures, for only about three grains are required for each plate, and the ounce contains 437 grains. This chemical is very poisonous, and it stains the fingers. But the fingers never need come into contact with it, if our directions are followed. A bone mustard spoon should be kept for the purpose of taking it out of its containing bottle.

Liquor Ammonia ·880 is the strongest solution of Ammonia that can be purchased. It quickly loses strength by exposure to the air, indeed it is not too much to say that it loses strength every time the stopper is removed from the bottle. For this reason only a small quantity should be purchased at a time, just sufficient to make up the formula required. The heat of the hand on the bottle is quite enough to set ff Ammonia in the form of gas, and for this reason the stopper should always be tied down, except when in actual use. Some adopt the plan of mixing the Ammonia at once with its bulk of water, and allowing for the addition in making up formulæ. But the best plan is to purchase just sufficient for present need.

Bromide of Potassium is in crystals, and is a stable compound. One ounce will be quite sufficient to begin with.

Alum (powdered). We recommend the reader to put a pound of it in a half gallon bottle, and to keep the bottle always full of water, adding water every time the bottle is drawn upon. This can be done until all the alum disappears from the bottom of the bottle, when more must be added. By this plan the water in the bottle will always be saturated, that is to say, it will contain as much alum in solution as it can hold.

Hyposulphite of Soda, which we will call hereafter "Hypo." for short, should be kept in a stone jar, in a dry place. While a most useful and indispensable salt in its proper place, it is a thing to be dreaded by the photographer should it get out of that place. Fingers which have touched "Hypo." must not touch plates, dishes, or anything else in the photographer's list until they have been well washed. The hypo. dish must be used for hypo. and nothing else. Indeed we may go further than this, and recommend that one particular dish should be used for each solution required.

The necessaries for developing beyond these chemicals comprise:—

    Three dishes,
    A good supply of water,
    Scales and weights,
    A graduated glass measure,
    A developing cup or glass.

Dish No. 1 is reserved for the developing solution, to be presently described. Dish No. 2, placed near it, is to cont. . a few ounces of the alum solution taken from the stock bottle. Dish No. 3—which may conveniently be double the size of the others, so as to be distinctive, and to have the further advantage of containing two plates at the same time—is for the hypo. solution—(hypo. 2½ ounces, water ½ pint). This dish, for the reason already given, may be placed at a respectful distance from the others. These dishes will then be placed on a table in front of the operator in the following order:—

| Hypo. Dish. | Alum Dish. | Developing Dish. |

We will now proceed to develope a plate, which we will suppose to have received the proper amount of exposure in the camera. Let us also suppose it to be a landscape subject, consisting of a liberal amount of sky, a few trees, and a foreground. Mix up the following solution, and place it in a small stoppered bottle, from which it can readily be poured drop by drop. It may be regarded as a stock solution, and will keep well if stoppered when not in use :—

 Bromide of Potassium ... ... 2 drachms.
 Water ... ... 4 ounces.
 Liquor Ammonia ... ... 2 ounces.

Let this bottle be labelled with a large **A** which can easily be discerned in the dim light of the dark room. The **A** will stand for accelerator, for this solution has the property of quickening the action of the developer. On the label, too, may be written the formula of the solution. This is a most convenient custom, and should be observed with all bottles in the laboratory.

We now proceed to spoon out 3 grains of pyrogallic acid into the developing cup. The first time or two we take the trouble to weigh out that quantity, but afterwards we can easily guess the amount by its bulk. Adding to this 2 ounces of water, we see that the pyro. quickly dissolves. Now add 4 drops of solution **A**, and the developer is ready. This amount of developer is quite sufficient for a 5 × 4 plate, particularly if the developing dish be of flat vulcanite, and of a size suitable to the plate developed. Of course if a large dish be used for a small plate, more developer must be needed to cover that plate. And the plate *must* be covered too, or stains are likely to result.

Taking the exposed plate from its double back, and keeping it at a safe distance from the red light, we place it in its dish, film side upwards, and immediately empty upon it the contents of the developing cup. This must be done in such a way that the liquid flows over the glass plate in one even wave. We may now put the cup aside and watch the gradual growth of the photographic image on the gelatine plate. This is always a pleasant, and most interesting sight. The plate when first wetted has a cream-colored surface, although it looks red enough under the light with which we are now working. No change occurs at once, but presently we see that part of the plate is rapidly darkening, while the extreme edges—which have been protected in the camera by the rebate of the dark slide—remain white as before. The darkening goes on, and now we see that the foliage of the trees—quite white—is projected upon the blackness. We recognize the dark part of the picture as the sky. It is the brightest thing in the landscape, and therefore it has had the greatest effect upon the sensitive surface in the camera, blackening a portion of that surface to a greater extent than could the light rays from any other part of the composition. But the picture is not only black and white: for now we find that silvery half-tones are making their appearance. These are found on the markings of the tree trunks, the various shades on a lichen-covered stone wall, and other objects. Still watching the gradual development of the picture, the action seems to hang fire a little. Now is the time to look to our accelerator (A solution) for further help. But we must not pour any direct into the dish, or it would have undue action on one part of the plate, and the negative would probably be spoilt. We therefore drop into the developing cup 6 drops of the solution, or thereabouts; empty the developer upon it, and immediately return the whole of the mixture to the dish. · The effect upon the picture is rapid. It quickly gains in strength, and unless care be taken the picture may be made too dense by allowing the action to go too far. The exact time when the developing process should be stopped, can only be learnt by experience. The beginner can, however, judge of the amount of density on the plate, by taking it out of the dish and holding it close to the ruby light so as to look through it. If indiarubber thumb and finger stalls be used, this can be done without soiling the hands. (It may be observed here that after the

development has commenced, the plate is not nearly so
sensitive to light as it was before. After, therefore,
the image has once begun to peep out, development
may be continued under quite a bright light, provided
that it is of an orange colour)

When it is judged that development is complete, and
when complete there should be very few white places
discernible upon the plate, the contents of the dish are
emptied into the sink, and the negative is well flushed
with water. Plenty of water at this stage, means a good
clear negative. After this the plate is put into the alum
dish for about 2 minutes, then it is ready for the fixing
operation in the hypo : dish.

Let us for a moment pause to see what this process
of fixation means. The plate originally consisted of a
film of bromide of silver mixed with gelatine. Only a
portion of this bromide has been utilized in making our
negative, and by the action of the light in the camera,
and subsequent development, this portion has been
darkened. But by far the larger mass of the film remains as unaltered bromide of silver; and by examining
the back of the developed plate, we can see the cream-
coloured film almost untouched by the chemicals we
have been using. This unaltered bromide causes the
plate not only to be opaque, but if allowed to remain,
would be infallibly darkened by light in the course of a
short time. So we must get rid of this bromide of
silver ; and the best way of doing so is to dissolve it out
of the film with hyposulphite of soda. We now see
why this chemical is called the fixing salt, and why it is
so prejudicial to the other photographic chemicals,
except in its own proper place. Before putting the
plate in the fixing bath it should be well rinsed under
the tap.

Under the action of the hypo. the plate gradually
loses its opacity, and becomes darker in appearance.
It should be left in the fixing bath for a few minutes
after the last trace of whiteness (bromide of silver)

has disappeared. It is then thoroughly washed under the tap, placed in a bath of clean water (which should be changed at intervals) for two or three hours, dried in a plate rack and the negative is finished.

The method of development which we have detailed is as simple as any, and will be found suitable to any plates in the market. Its fault, if it have one, is that the pyrogallic acid is used dry, and being of a light woolly nature, it is apt to fly about, and contaminate other things in the room. Mixed with water alone it will only keep good for a few hours. If a good batch of plates have to be developed, it is the best plan perhaps to mix up the whole quantity of pyrogallic acid needed, and to measure off so much for each plate. Here is an alternative method of working by which the contents of a one ounce bottle of pyrogallic acid can at once be made into a solution which will keep good for months. In 8 ounces of water put 20 drops of nitric acid, and pour the mixture upon 1 ounce of pyrogallic acid. Eight drops of this stock solution will then contain 1 grain of pyrogallic, so that a developer can be quickly made up from it.

Hitherto we have considered only the case of a plate which has received the proper amount of exposure in the camera. With such a plate all is plain sailing. It developes itself as it were, and requires little attention beyond watching to see when the action must be stopped. But in the hands of a beginner, plates do not behave at first in this convenient manner. They are either under or over exposed, and the photographic aspirant is at first quite at a loss to know which error of these two he has committed. We will endeavour to enlighten him. An under exposed plate may be looked for after exposure in dull weather, or when the camera has been used late in the afternoon, when the sun has lost much of its power. If one plate out of a batch taken at the same time, and under the same conditions, turns out to be under-exposed; let the other plates be allowed to rest for three weeks or a month before they are developed. Strange as it may seem, there is a kind of continuing action of the light on a plate which has been once exposed, although that plate be subsequently kept in darkness. This continuing action will cause an under-exposed plate to ripen, so that eventually, after a rest like that suggested, it will yield a good negative.

"But how," it may be asked, "is a beginner to know whether a plate has been under-exposed." Simply by its behaviour under development. The sky will come out very slowly, and very little else will appear. Dose after dose of "accelerator" may be added to the plate, but nothing seems to hasten it. If washed and fixed, it will consist of nothing but black sky and clear glass. Of course this is an extreme case. Under-exposure generally may be detected by the slowness with which the image makes its appearance, and the hardness of the contrasts between the lights and the shadows of the picture. There is no remedy for this state of things. The best thing to do under the circumstances, is to scratch the film across with the finger-nail, in case the operator should be afterwards tempted to print from such a production.

Over exposure is a more common fault, and this is fortunate, for the fault can be remedied to a great extent during the developing operation. Over-exposure is evidenced by the image flashing out on all parts or the plate at the same instant. The plate darkens all at once, and will speedily become one black mass unless a remedy be applied. Should this sudden flashing out of the picture occur, at once throw off the developer, and flood the plate with water from the tap. Now mix up some fresh developer, containing only one-third of the usual quantity of ammonia solution, and with a few drops of a ten per cent. solution of bromide of potassium added. This salt has a restraining action, as will be very soon apparent. A bottle containing it should be kept for such emergencies, and should be compounded thus:—

      Bromide of potassium, ½ ounce.
      Water . . . 5 ounces.

By such precautions an over-exposed plate may be developed into a decent negative. But let it always be remembered that nothing is equal to a properly exposed plate. An over-exposed one will generally require intensifying, a process that will be described later on.

Many other alkalies besides ammonia are used with pyrogallic acid as a developer, and although ammonia is most commonly used, the idea is gaining ground that it can be usefully supplanted by some of the others. It has the disadvantage of causing a plate to be discoloured if more than a certain quantity be used, which is commonly the case if the development be at all forced when under-exposure is being corrected. The two alkalies most often used in place of ammonia, are the carbonate of soda, and the carbonate of potash. We will first of all describe a very good developer compounded with carbonate of soda, $i.e.$ common washing soda, not the bi-carbonate, which is often miscalled carbonate of soda. In a quart bottle, put washing soda ¼ lb., and fill up with warm water. Add 12 grains of bromide of potassium. For use take pyrogallic acid as before, pour upon it one ounce of water, and one ounce of the soda solution. Here we have a developer which yields first-class results. It has no smell, and the soda being a stable salt, a large quantity of solution can be mixed at once, for it keeps well. As in the case of ammonia, the alkali acts as an accelerator, and it must be diminished or increased as circumstances require. Carbonate of potash has lately come into extreme favour under the name of Beach's developer; for the popular way of using it must be attributed to Mr. Beach, of New York. The following method of making the developer has lately been published in several photographic periodicals, and it gives, when so compounded, the very best results.

Make two solutions:—

No. 1.—Pyro. Solution.
Warm Water ... ... 2 ounces
Sulphite Soda ... ... 2 ounces
When cold add
Sulphurous Acid ... ... 2 ounces
Pyrogallic Acid ... ... ½ ounce

No. 2.—Potash Solution.
A   Water ... ... 4 ounces
    Carbonate Potash... ... 3 ounces
B   Warm Water ... ... 3 ounces
    Sulphite Soda ... ... 2 ounces

Combine A and B. These two solutions keep well.

To develope, add to each ounce of water, 1 dram of No. 1 Solution, and ¾ dram of No. 2 Solution. This is weaker than Mr. Beach's formula, and it is best to commence developing with a still further dilution from two-thirds as strong, to even one-third, if over-exposure be suspected beforehand.

It cannot be too weak, and, indeed, I take it as a good test of the suitability of its strength, if the developer begin to act in from half-a-minute to a minute. If any earlier signs are visible, the water jug must be handy. Quantity is of less consequence than promptness.

As long as the very slowest progress is being made do not add potash, but when action ceases, about ¼ dram may be added at a time, and in case the developer has had too much of a drenching to check it, then add pyro. also. Don't be impatient if five, or even ten minutes are occupied in development. Develope blacker than with ammonia, indeed until only the unaffected shades can be seen. If the development be too rapid, especially at first, a loss of half-tones or intermediate shades will result, giving a harsh print showing great contrasts. The same developer can be used half-a dozen times, or more, for all I know. The secret of success lies in full exposure and slow development. If too dense, the negative can be reduced without deterioration. The mode of doing this will be explained later on.

So much for alkaline development, which, in one form or other, is the most favoured method of rendering the latent photographic image visible. We will now describe a totally different system, which is little practised in this country, but is almost universally used on the Continent. It is known as Ferrous Oxalate Development. It has the merit of not staining the fingers, and for this reason it should be a favourite with ladies. It also possesses the advantage of permitting a dozen or more negatives to be developed in the same batch of developer. Its disadvantage lies in the difficulty of increasing or decreasing its power in cases of over or under-exposure. Those who use it, therefore, should be careful to make their exposures right.

Take

    Neutral Oxalate of Potash ... 1 lb.
    Boiling Water... ... ... 1 quart.

This solution should be mixed in a basin, and should be constantly stirred until all the crystals are dissolved. It may then be set aside to cool. When cold, it is ready for use, and may be bottled off as a stock solution, to be drawn upon when it is desired to develope a few plates. For use, take 2 ounces of this stock solution, and add to it 1 dram of protosulphate of iron *in powder*. Stir for a minute with a glass rod, and then add a drop or two of your bromide of potash solution. Having washed the plate to be developed in a dish of clean water for a minute, it can be transferred to a dish containing the developer. The action is much slower than in the case of alkaline development; but when once the image makes its appearance, it speedily gains density, and development may be carried on until nearly the whole surface of the plate appears black. The colour of the finished negative is not yellow, like an ammonia developed plate, but is black, like one developed with potash. One great advantage in this is, that the after operation of printing is very much shortened.

If a negative has become extremely yellow under ammonia development, or if it be stained by excess of ammonia, a few minutes immersion in the following clearing solution will speedily remedy the defect.

CLEARING SOLUTION.

Alum ... ... 2 ounces.
Citric Acid ... ... 1 ounce.
Water ... ... ½ pint.

Extreme yellowness is also a legacy often left by the carbonate of soda developer. This is better remedied by a clearing solution containing iron. The formula is as follows:—

Alum ... ... ½ ounce.
Citric Acid ... ... ½ ounce.
Sulphate of Iron ... ... 1½ ounces.
Water ... ... ½ pint.

The decolouring property of this solution is remarkable, and the negative comes from it with a bloom upon it which is a pleasure to behold. The shadows are cleared, and the dark portions of the film are turned to pearly grey.

It has been already pointed out that an under-exposed negative is not worth keeping. An over-exposed one is very often benefitted by the operation known as intensification. This is the formula:—

Mercuric Chloride ... ... 1 ounce.
Sal Ammoniac ... ... 1 ounce.
Water ... ... 12 ounces.

This mixture is a deadly poison, and the bottle containing it should be kept in some corner where it is not likely to be meddled with. A negative can be intensified with it long after it has been fixed, washed, and dried. In any case the negative to be treated should be placed in water to which a little alum has been added for some hours previous to the operation.

If any hypo. remains in the film, the mercury will do more harm than good. Having taken this precaution, immerse the negative in a clean dish, pour upon it sufficient of the mercury solution to cover it, and keep the dish gently rocking, until the image is perfectly bleached. This will take place in about two minutes. Now wash the plate most thoroughly under the tap, and put it in a bath of the following, which may be kept like the mercury as a stock solution:—

   Soda Sulphite ... ... 1 ounce.
   Water ... ... 10 ounces.

In this solution the snow-white image will speedily turn black. When the action is complete the negative must have a final rinse under the tap, and we can then examine it. We shall find that the thin image has become dense, and that what before was a mere ghost, although possessing plenty of detail, is now a good printable negative. Still, let us once more remember that intensification is at the best but a makeshift, and that careful exposure in the first instance will give a far better result.

If a negative is so dense that it becomes difficult for the light to penetrate it in the after process of printing, it has probably been over-developed. It can be easily reduced by the following method. Make a saturated solution of the red prussiate of potash. Also make up a fresh bath of fixing solution (hypo.) of the usual strength. Add 10 drops of the former to the latter, and place your negative in the mixture. Reduction will immediately commence. When it ceases, and if the negative should be still too dense, add another 10 drops of the prussiate and commence afresh. Repeat this again and again until the required density is arrived at.

It now only remains to varnish the negative. This should on no account be ommitted if the negative be valued. The varnish forms a protecting film to the negative which keeps out damp and other destructive influences. For this operation we require proper varnish, an empty dry bottle, and a pneumatic holder. Putting a plate on the holder we gently warm it in front of a clear fire. It must be only warm, not hot. Now pour a pool of varnish in the centre of the glass and by tipping the plate urge it to one corner after the other. Pour off the surplus into the dry bottle, rock the plate from side to side, hold it in front of the fire until it gets thoroughly hot, and the operation is complete. The negative is now ready for yielding prints upon paper. A description of the process will form the subject of our next chapter.

PRINTING FROM THE NEGATIVE.

THE work of printing is one in which amateurs as a rule do not excel. The reason for this is that it not only requires a liberal amount of patience, which in these go-a-head times is a virtue not much cultivated, but because it comprises a number of operations full of little details, each one of which must have careful attention. These operations include exposure of sensitive paper under the negative to daylight; the toning of the positive image thus obtained, its fixation, and last but not least, a thorough washing by which the fixing salt is thoroughly eliminated.

The apparatus required is simple. Printing frames, one or two dishes, and three large earthenware pans, being all the things that are necessary, beyond a plentiful supply of water. Sensitised silver paper can now be bought at a very cheap rate, cheaper indeed than one can make it, if he only counts the cost of the necessary chemicals, to say nothing of the time occupied in its preparation which would be considerable. With the paper ready to hand, bought in a sensitised condition ready for the printing frame, the worker has merely to provide himself with the chemicals for toning and fixing. For toning he will want a small quantity of acetate of soda, or borax, according to the formula which he prefers, and a fifteen-grain tube of gold. A tube of this size will tone several dozens of small pictures. To ensure success in printing—and it is by the general brightness and colour of these prints that your competence as a photographer will be guaged by friends—

the greatest care must be taken to keep all solutions separate. This is easily done if care be taken to complete each portion of the work before the next stage be entered upon. Thus the exposures will be made as they must be in the daytime, then when the light begins to fade the toning may be commenced. When this part of the business is complete, and not till then, the fixing solution (which is merely a solution of hypo.) may be mixed, and the prints submitted to its influence. A careless worker who places his toning bath next to his fixing bath and allows fingers or splashes to travel from one to the other, at once spoils his work. Again, with the dishes—one dish should be set apart rigidly for toning purposes and should be used for that purpose only; and it is as well, although not quite so important, that the fixing salt should have its own particular dish. With these preliminary, but by no means unnecessary words of caution, we can proceed to give a detailed account of the printing operations.

EXPOSURE IN THE PRINTING FRAME.

THE photographic printing frame is made of wood, generally teak, and can be bought in the usual sizes of plates. The negative fits into a rebate, and is placed in position film side upwards. Upon this a piece of sensitive paper previously cut to size, is laid with its shiny albumenized surface touching the surface of the film. A few folds of clean blotting paper or a pad of felt is next placed above the paper, and then the hinged back of the printing frame covers up the entire arrangement. The two metal springs are now brought over and placed in position, and all is ready for exposure to the active rays of the sun. The hinged back is so arranged that by displacing one of the springs, half of the back board can be folded over, and the paper can be examined in a dull light so as to watch the progress of printing.

D

A novel kind of printing frame has been recently introduced which is known as Durnford's printing frame. It is shown at page 127. Many will be attracted by its small volume, which renders it especially valuable to those who prefer to carry their printing requisites from place to place with them. It consists of a hinged board covered with cloth. At the back, not shown in the wood-cuts, are two springs, provided at each end with stirrup-shaped catches, which can be bent over to clutch the negative placed upon the board. The stirrups are furnished with rubber cushions to obviate any chance of breaking the glass. A sheet of sensitive paper is put between the negative and the board. In the cut, one pair of stirrups has been released, so that the print can be examined in the same way as in the more common form of frame.

As in the taking of a negative no fixed rule can be given as to the time of exposure, but in the one case it is a matter of seconds, and in the other it may be a question of hours. The time will depend upon the density and the colour of the negative, and also upon the available light. A black and white negative with cool grey half-tones, such as ferrous oxalate gives, will print on a favourable day in about fifteen minutes. A negative treated by ammonia or soda development, may require double that time, for the colour of the film is of a less actinic quality. On a dull day, again, the first named negative may require an hour's exposure or more. and of course the other negative will require under the same conditions a proportionate increase in the time of exposure. A poor thin negative will never give a really good print, but by modifying the amount of light submitted to it, a much better result can be obtained than if it were treated as a thoroughly good one. Indeed, the amount of light allowed to fall upon the printing frame must in all cases depend upon the nature of the negative. Never must the direct rays of the sun be employed unless the negative be of quite exceptional density, and when therefore a print cannot be otherwise obtained. Diffused daylight must be the rule, that is to say, the printing frames must be exposed where only the reflected rays from the open sky can reach them ; as, for instance, on some support such as a window ledge on the shady side of a house. A thin negative may be exposed in the same position, but it should be protected by a covering of red or yellow tissue paper, so that the printing action is rendered much slower. The same result can be obtained by giving it a long exposure inside a room, at some distance from the window.

In any case the action must be watched by folding back the half of the back printing frame as already indicated. And in all cases the action should be allowed to continue until the print looks far more deeply printed than would be desirable in a finished picture. The reason of this is, that the image loses much of its force in the subsequent operations.

It is not worth while to undertake the necessary, and all times somewhat tedious operations of printing, toning, and fixing for one or two pictures, for the work involved is much the same if a single print or several dozen are taken in hand at the same time. And although, for the sake of simplicity, we will write as if only a single print were in question, it must be understood that our remarks apply to a batch. Let a fine day be chosen for the work, or it will prove tedious indeed, and let at least three or four printing frames be employed, according to the number of negatives upon which the operator is at work. One word more, do not attempt to print while other work is going on, or several prints will be left to themselves too long, and will be over printed.

TONING.

WHEN the print is removed from the frame it is of a dark red colour, very different from the tint of an ordinary finished photograph. To correct this, and to give it a more pleasing colour, is the object of the toning bath. Previous to immersion in this bath, the print must be washed in one or two changes of water. This need not be done in darkness, but must be done in a subdued light, such as would be afforded by a room with the blind drawn down. As a further precaution, the pan in which the print is placed, may be covered with a tray, or dark cloth. A ten minutes soaking in one pan, a change of water, and a further ten minutes will be sufficient. The print will then be ready for the toning bath.

Formula I.

Acetate of Soda ... ... 20 grains.
Distilled Water ... ... 8 ounces.
Gold Solution (see under) 1 drachm.

For all toning formulæ the gold is most conveniently used as a solution prepared as follows. Nick the tube of gold in the centre with a fine file, and after breaking it between the fingers over a sheet of clean writing paper, transfer both gold and broken glass to a two ounce bottle containing 15 drachms of distilled water. Each drachm of water will then contain one grain or chloride of gold. This should be labelled "Gold Solution." The quantity of toning solution given above, should be sufficient to tone one whole sheet of paper, one grain of gold being generally calculated to do this amount of toning. Should the cut prints in the aggregate amount to more than a sheet, the amount of solution must be increased proportionately. The toning solution must now be poured into the toning dish, and one or two prints immersed therein at a time. One print should not be allowed to overlap another while in this bath, or the toning will be unequal. The dish should too be occasionally rocked, and the prints kept on the move by changing places with one another. A change of colour is soon apparent. When the prints are first taken from their washing water they are of an ugly brick red tone. This gradually changes to crimson, and from crimson to purple. The prints should not be removed until every trace of red has disappeared. To ascertain when this is the case raise the print gently from the solution and look through it. The toning operation is conveniently conducted in a room with a yellow blind, which can be occasionally drawn aside for a moment, in order that the colour of the prints may be examined. As each print is finished, place it in a pan of water, and supply its place in the toning bath by a fresh one. The acetate bath must be mixed two days before use. This is important. It will keep well, provided that it is placed when not in use in a stone bottle, where white light cannot reach it. It must be strengthened for subsequent use by extra gold, the amount of which will depend upon the calls made upon it, as already indicated.

Here is another toning formula, which must be used as soon as prepared. It will not keep, but it is useful in cases of emergency.

Bicarbonate of Soda ... 3 grains.
Water ... ... 8 ounces.
Gold Solution ... ... 1 drachm.

For warmer tones, the following is recommended:—

Phosphate of Soda ... 30 grains.
Water ... ... 8 ounces.
Gold Solution ... ... 1 drachm.

The borax toning bath is a general favourite, and it seems to work particularly well with ready prepared sensitive paper, such as we have recommended the beginner to use. Here is the method of preparation.

In a pint jug place 90 grains of borax, and upon it pour 15 ounces (three quarters of a pint) of boiling water. Stir with a glass rod until the borax is dissolved. Put this solution aside until it has become almost cold, then add two drachms of gold solution. If this bath be used, and we can most highly recommend it as an efficient one, the prints need not be printed so deeply as for other toning formulæ.

When all the prints have been duly toned, they should be passed through one or two changes of water, the toning dish is carefully put away, and we may proceed to compound the fixing bath thus :—

    Hyposulphite of Soda ... $\frac{1}{2}$ lb.
    Warm Water ... ... 1 quart.
    Liquor Ammonia ... ... 20 drops.

This fixing bath is best mixed in a deep dish, and as soon as the crystals are dissolved, the toned prints may be placed therein, one by one. When all are in, the bottom one may be moved to the top, then the next one to it may be moved, and so on until they have all changed places. This movement allows the solution free access to each print in turn. In fifteen minutes the fixation should be complete.

Now comes the washing process, upon the efficiency of which permanence of results so much depends. Let two large pans of clean water be provided. Remove each print separately from the soda solution, and place in pan No. 1. Then force the mass of prints with the open hand to the bottom of the vessel, and pour off the water into the sink. Stand the pan on its edge for five minutes for the prints to drain. Then fill up with fresh water. Now transfer the pictures to pan No. 2, and go through the same process. Gradually increase the time for which the prints are allowed to soak, and finally let them soak in a fresh supply of water all night. A further change in the morning will finish the washing process.

The prints may now be dried between folds of clean blotting paper, their edges trimmed, and they are then ready to be mounted on card, or in an album.

It is best however to trim the prints before toning, because they are best mounted while in a damp state. If the trimming be left until after toning, the prints must be dried, for they cannot be cut wet, and they have again to be damped for mounting. This represents therefore a needless waste of time.

The best way to trim prints is to use a glass cutting shape sold for the purpose, and to cut upon a piece of plate glass. The print is placed face upwards on the glass plate, and the cutting glass placed above it. Through the upper glass the picture can be seen, and care must be taken that any straight lines in it, such as will occur in an architectural subject, are parallel with the edge of the cutting glass. A sharp knife is now run along each side of the cutting glass, and the ragged edges of the print are cleanly separated from it.

The best mounting material is perhaps good starch paste used cold. A hog hair stencil brush will break up the lumps of paste on the damp paper, and after allowing the pasted print to rest for a couple of minutes, it may be carefully transferred to the cardboard mount, and pressed down with a clean handkerchief. The appearance of a mounted photograph is much improved, if a double or single line of red ink be drawn with a pen all round its edge, at a distance say of a quarter of an inch from the margin of the picture. Professional photographers always roll their prints after mounting, and have a proper press for the purpose. For a small sum many will undertake to roll a few prints when required to do so.

INSTANTANEOUS PICTURES.

One of the most noticeable features of modern dry plates is their intense rapidity. When a non-photographer reads that certain pictures of trotting horses have been taken in the 2,000th part of a second, he is apt to smile with incredulity. But he must be convinced in spite of himself that there is no exaggeration in the statement, if he be shown one of the many photographs which have been taken of lightning flashes. The duration of time represented by a flash of lightning is something infinitely less than the 2,000th part of a second. But such pictures are, at the best, but scientific curiosities, although they prove most conclusively the intensely rapid manner in which a gelatine plate can be affected by the access of light.

Most beginners will not be content until they have tried their 'prentice hands at instantaneous work, although, possibly, they will soon learn that slower pictures which give more time for their consideration and general treatment, are as a rule far more satisfactory in the end. Still there are many subjects—such as sea-scapes with shipping, animal studies, including children (pardon us, fond parents) which must be taken instantaneously, or not at all.

For instantaneous work the hand is not quick enough to uncap and recap the lens. A piece of apparatus called an instantaneous shutter, is therefore employed to do this work automatically. Their number is legion, and the different designs show what a marvellous amount of skill has been expended upon this one item of the photographic outfit. We will content ourselves with noticing one or two forms of shutter only, but they may be regarded as being among the best in the market. First of all let us describe the "Phantom" shutter, shown at page 107. It consists of a light but strong frame of ebonite, with an aperture at the lower part, which fits the hood of the lens employed. In front of this aperture is a flap which can be either gently raised by the thumbscrew shown on the left hand side of the drawing, or can be suddenly released by touching the catch shown below. For non-instantaneous exposures, that is to say for all ordinary work, this shuttter can be usefully employed. The flap is slowly raised so that the dark foreground gets, as it should do, more exposure than the bright sky which acts so much more quickly upon the plate. When the flap is raised to a certain height, a shutter working in a grove suddenly falls behind it, and the exposure is terminated. For instantaneous effects the instrument is used in a somewhat different manner. An elastic band, shown in the cut, is fastened to the shutter and frame respectively, so that the descent of the former is rapid in the extreme. The tension of the rubber band also affects the flap which has a tendency to fly open unless held back by its catch. Directly this catch is turned to one side, or pulled to one side by an attached string, as shown in page 127, the flap flies up, and the shutter falls down.

The "Phantom" is rendered still more efficient by a mechanical attachment. This consists of a little pneumatic piston, with a tiny piston rod, which takes the place of the catch shown in page 127. In communication with the piston is a tube, which may be of any convenient length, terminated by an india-rubber air-ball. Pressure of this air-ball in the hand causes a force of wind to rush through the tube to the piston, the little rod is forced back, and the shutter does its work. It may be mentioned that this pneumatic attachment is the means adopted for working many other forms of shutters, one of which will be next described.

The "Right-about-turn" shutter (see two Figs. on page 127) has a certain likeness to the "Phantom," but it has the merit of being one half the size. It is thus described by the makers who claim that it is the lightest and smallest shutter made. "One screen opens as flap in exposing, then falls back upside down as a drop shutter in closing, giving foreground the longest exposure. The length of exposure is under complete control, slow or quick action being obtained either by pnuematic action or hand lever." One Fig. shows the first part of this action. The shutter has been released, and the flap is rising, slowly or quickly as the case may be. In the other it has risen completely and is commencing its downward drop so as to terminate the exposure.

In the "Economic" shutter (page 127) we have a flap which opens and closes again by a crank action with great smoothness and rapidity. The simplicity, as well as the small bulk of this contrivance must quickly render it a favourite. Even with the most compact apparatus, the tourist likes to reduce the weight of his necessaries as much as possible. The adoption of an instantaneous shutter which can be carried in his waistcoat pocket will be a sore temptation to him.

LANTERN PICTURES.

The magic lantern has long been a favourite instrument with children, and under past conditions, when the pictures thrown by it were hand painted, and were little better than rough daubs; it was only fit for the amusement of children. But now that photography is able to furnish pictures full of the most exquisite detail, pictures which are actually improved by being greatly magnified, the lantern takes a far more important place, and is at once raised to the position of a scientific apparatus of the greatest value. With the improved pictures too has come an improved instrument (see page 136). The old oil lamp, with its disagreeable smell, and its weak light, has given place to a lamp with three or four wicks burning mineral oil. The lenses too are now made on scientific principles, and for a small sum we can purchase a lantern fit for exhibition purposes. We may look forward to the time when every household will regard a lantern as a necessity, and even now they are by no means uncommon. Without question every amateur photographer should possess one. During the long winter evenings when other photographic operations are impossible, he can print from his negatives slides for the lantern, which with ordinary precautions will compare favourably with any that he can purchase at shops. We will now give plain directions by which this branch of photographic work can be readily accomplished.

For the production of slides we shall require some gelatine plates measuring $3\frac{1}{4} \times 3\frac{1}{4}$ inches. This is the standard size of all lantern pictures, and no other size should be thought of. The plates ordinarily used for negatives will answer the purpose, and if the size cannot readily be obtained, quarter plates can be used. These measure $4\frac{1}{4} \times 3\frac{1}{4}$ inches, so that an inch must be cut off either before the plate is used, or after it is finished. An American glass cutter can be used for this, but a diamond is, of course, better. Having chosen some suitable negatives, which may be on quarter plates, or even 5×4 plates, place one in a printing frame, with the film side up, just as if you were about to print a proof on albumenized paper. But instead of paper place above the negative one of the square plates just mentioned. By holding this against the negative, and holding the latter close to the red lamp, it is easy to choose that portion of the subject which it is most desirable to reproduce as a transparency, the negative being dimly seen through the plate. Now carefully replace on the table, and fasten in the back of the frame in the usual way. All is now ready for exposure. Daylight being far too intense for the purpose, we must use some kind of artificial light, and the most convenient is gas. If possible, have a table gas lamp with a good batswing burner. Light this before commencing operations, and turn it down to "the blue." (A capital burner is now made on purpose for photographers. It cannot be turned quite out, and is always ready when it is wanted.) Now hold the printing frame so that the negative faces the burner, at a distance of about 18 inches from it. Turn up the light for three seconds, and immediately turn it down again. This exposure will be about sufficient for a good negative, and using a gelatine plate of ordinary rapidity. If the negative be thin, place it three feet away from the light, and increase the exposure four fold. If, on the contrary, the negative be very dense, it may be placed much closer to the light; as in other branches of photography, the exact exposure can only be learnt by experience. At the same time it is all important that correct exposure should be given for each negative employed.'

There are several methods by which transparencies may be developed, indeed any developer can be used, if we are not particular as to colour. The ordinary pyrogallic and ammonia developer will give a picture of a disagreeable yellow tinge, and although this tint can be partly removed by a clearing solution of citric acid and alum, the colour remaining is not satisfactory when the picture is seen on the screen. If pyrogallic developing is used at all, it should be employed in the form of the Beach developer already described. This gives a good black colour. Almost as good a result can be promised by using the soda developer. But this mode of development is specially liable to extreme yellowness, particularly if the operation be prolonged. It must therefore be followed by using the clearing solution containing iron, which has been already given in the chapter on development. This solution should be freshly mixed for the purpose.

The developer which in the writer's hands has given the best results for transparency work, is a modification of the ferrous oxalate method. Mix the developer as already recommended, by adding the powdered iron crystals to the oxalate of potash solution, and then adding a few drops of bromide of potash solution. So far we have the ferrous oxalate developer pure and simple, which may be used as it is. Here comes the modification. Mix as a stock solution the following :—

Citric Acid ... ... 5 ounces.
Distilled, or Rain Water... 20 ounces.
Liquor Ammonia ('880)... 2 ounces.

The citric acid crystals may conveniently be rubbed down in a mortar. Add the water to them, and after transferring the mixture to a strong bottle, add the ammonia. This last addition will cause the evolution of so much heat that the crystals left unpowdered will quickly dissolve. If the solution be kept beyond a few weeks, a kind of mouldy fungoid growth will be observed in it. This can be prevented by adding to the solution when first mixed, a pinch of salicylic acid in powder. Doubtless, a drop of carbolic acid or a few cloves would answer the same purpose. This solution may be labelled "citrate of ammonia." The modified developer is made by mixing the solution of citrate of ammonia with the ferrous oxalate developer in equal parts.

In making transparencies we must be as particular in keeping the hypo. solution at a respectful distance, as we must be during the operation of toning prints. And this is best achieved by not mixing any hypo. until all the transparencies which are in hand are ready for fixing. Let the operations be conducted as follows.

In the first place clear the operating table of everything not actually required for the business in hand. On the operator's right hand let the gas-lamp be in readiness turned down to its very lowest. At the back of the table should stand the red lamp supported at a convenient height upon some form or stand. Immediately in front of it should be placed the developing dish, and a half plate ebonite one is the best for the purpose. It has the merit of having a flat bottom, and it is large enough to hold two plates side by side. This is a great convenience in transparency work, for the reason that sometimes through injudicious exposure a plate will require much persuasion before it will yield up a good image. It may remain in the developer for ten minutes or more without detriment, while other more obliging plates are being finished in the same dish.

At the left hand side of the developing dish should stand a large dish capable of holding a dozen or two lantern slides. This should be filled with a weak solution of alum and water. As each plate is developed, it should be washed well, and transferred to the alum bath. In this bath the plates can remain for many hours if required, without suffering any harm; of course they must not see daylight for they are still in a sensitive condition, but an occasional gleam of gaslight such as they would get while other plates are being exposed, will do them no harm whatever. If one plate is being exposed to light while another remains in the developing dish, the latter should be covered over with a piece of card or the lid of a cardboard plate box.

After all the plates of a batch are developed and in the alum bath, we can proceed to fix them in hypo. solution. This should be mixed freshly for the purpose. Indeed, it should be a standard rule with photographers to mix this salt freshly for whatever purpose it may be required. The soda is so cheap now-a-days that economy in its use need not be thought about.

The dish used for the fixing solution should be large enough to contain at least four lantern slides at one time. As each is cleared it may be rinsed and put back in the alum dish until all are so replaced. Then take the large dish to the sink, carefully empty away the alum and water, and let the tap run into it for some minutes, every now and then tilting up the dish as the water accumulates. Finally, let the plates remain in water for at least a couple of hours, and then proceed to examine them. If the iron developer has been used, a slight deposit of oxalate of lime may possibly be noticeable on the surface of the film, making it somewhat milky in appearance. This is often of such a superficial nature that it can be wiped off with a tuft of cotton wool, while the water from the tap is allowed to run upon the plate. But if the disease is of a deeper nature and seems to attack the body of the film, more energetic measures must be resorted to for its cure. Mix the following :—

Saturated Solution of Alum ... 10 ounces.
Sulphuric Acid ... ... $\frac{1}{2}$ ounce.

Pour this mixture on and off the plate two or three times, and the milkiness will at once disappear. This strongly acid solution will have, with some plates, a tendency to cause them to frill, so that it must be used with caution. But in most cases the application of a tuft of cotton wool will do what is necessary. If the acid be used the plates must undergo another careful washing, but if not, they can be rinsed under a tap, and placed in a rack to dry spontaneously. On a fine day they will dry quickest in the open air, but should be placed in some situation where wind and dust cannot do them any injury.

In developing transparencies the all important point is to arrive at the proper amount of density. This amount must depend upon the purpose for which the transparency is required. For an ordinary lantern picture the development should be allowed to continue until the picture appears to be rather overdone. Its real density may be better judged by holding it up to the red lamp once or twice during development, and viewing it by transmitted light. If it does not appear deep enough, return it once more to the dish until the right amount of density is attained.

But the transparency may be wanted merely as a vehicle for obtaining another negative, or for enlarging purposes. In these cases the development must be carried to a much greater extent, and every bit of detail must be dragged out before the plate can be considered complete. The same rule must guide the operator, if his transparencies are intended for window decoration. These, it must be remembered, will be viewed when finished, by transmitted light, and can be therefore made very dense indeed. We may state in passing, that there is a very wide field open to the photographer in this direction. Good transparencies backed up with ground glass, and perhaps leaded together with a frame of tinted cathedral glass, have a splendid effect when used as door panels, fan-lights, or in ordinary windows.

Hitherto, in dealing with the production of lantern slides, we have supposed that the negative employed is of such a size that it can be reproduced as a positive by contact printing in the ordinary printing frame,

Occasionally, however, the operator will have a negative of larger size which he will be anxious to reduce to the standard lantern size. Let us suppose, for instance, that he has a whole-plate negative ($8\frac{1}{2} \times 6\frac{1}{2}$ inches) and that he requires to reduce this to lantern size ($3\frac{1}{4}$ inches square). It is quite plain that the contact method will not do here, unless he requires but a quarter of the negative to be reproduced. The reduction must be made by means of the camera, with such additions as any amateur worker can arrange for himself in a very short time.

Upon a deal table nail a couple of laths at such a distance apart that the camera will slide to and fro between them, like a tramcar on its rails. At one end of this miniature railway, place a small lidless box—a packing case will do—with its open end facing the camera. In the bottom of this box a hole should be cut ($8\frac{1}{2} \times 6\frac{1}{2}$ inches) to fit the negative. A groove top and bottom, made by nailing slips of wood on the outside of the opening, will hold the negative in position. Outside the box place a sheet of stout card at an angle of 45 degrees, so that the light from the sky is reflected through the negative. (We are to suppose that the work is being carried on out of doors, or at any rate in some kind of glass-house.) Between the open box and the camera, and on the upper part of each lay a couple of light wooden rods, and over these put a dark cloth. We must now see to the camera. If it be larger than quarter size, the ground glass screen should have pencilled upon it a $3\frac{1}{4}$ inch square, as a guide to the size of the picture required. The dark slide too must be furnished with a carrier to hold a $3\frac{1}{4}$ inch plate. The lens employed should be of short focus, the wide angled doublet, or portable symetrical, shown at Fig. 21, being suitable for the purpose. A rapid rectilinear, or a portrait lens can be used, but neither of these will give quite such good results as the one just recommended.

E

The picture must be carefully focussed, using the largest stop in the rotating diaphragm. In this, great advantage will be found in using a focussing glass, which can be purchased for a few shillings. The glass is held touching the ground glass screen of the camera, and the eye is applied to the smaller end of the brass tube in which it is mounted. A good focus can be more quickly obtained by means of this glass than with the unaided eye. By moving the camera to and fro between the laths nailed to the table, and by working the focussing screw of the camera, it will be found easy to get the image on the screen down to the correct size.

With regard to the exposure necessary to ensure the best results, we must once more speak rather vaguely. It depends upon the light, the density and colour or the negative, and the lens employed. But supposing that the light be good, and to consist of the reflected light from a clear blue sky, that we employ the smallest stop but one of the portable symmetrical lens, and that we are using a first-rate whole-plate negative, with a fairly rapid plate in our dark slide, the exposure will be about two minutes.

Lantern slides after being dried do not require much further treatment. If used uncoloured they ought to be varnished in the same way that a negative is varnished. Coloured pictures are protected by the medium used as a vehicle by the painter, which consists of thin varnish. In any case they will require to be mounted with a thin cover glass, and between the two glasses is placed a paper mask. These masks are made of black paper and can be bought ready cut with a round, square, or cushioned-shaped opening. A landscape will generally look best in a round mask, but occasionally when a figure is standing at one side of the picture part of it might be cut off by that shaped opening, in which case a cushioned-shaped mask must be employed. For architectural subjects the square mask is most suitable.

The two glasses with their intervening mask must now be bound together by a slip of gummed paper. The black paper known as needle paper is the best to employ, and the gum which sticks most firmly to glass, is made as follows :—
Dextrine ... ... 1 ounce.
Loaf Sugar ... ... ½ ounce.
Mix into a mucilage with warm water, and leave on the hob for an hour or two until thoroughly transparent. One side of the needle paper should be gummed with this mixture, and when dry the paper can be cut into strips ⅜ths of an inch wide and 14 inches long.

To bind a slide with one of these gummed slips, damp the gummed side of the paper with a sponge or with the tongue, and place it before you on the table. Now take a lantern slide and place one edge of it at the end of the strip, and exactly in its centre. Now turn it over and over on the strip until all four edges are covered, and in the meantime press down the edges of the paper so that they will lap over, and fasten the two pieces of glass rigidly together.

Some kind of slide holder is required before the pictures can be shown in the lantern. Professional exhibitors use a separate mahogany frame for each picture and the picture remains in it. But for amateurs this plan is needlessly expensive. A good plan is to employ what is called a panoramic slide holder, which consists of a frame having a groove at the top and bottom, through which the pictures can be passed in turn, one picture pushing out the other which has been already shown.

There is also another slide holder which can be well recommended. This consists of a frame to fit the lantern, within which slides a double holder, with places for two pictures. While one picture is being shown the other is outside the lantern, and can be changed for the one next in order.

A well executed photograph on glass, prepared for the

lantern, is a photograph at its very best. A picture of the same size on paper would in comparison give a very poor effect, for the grain of the paper destroys in a measure the finer details. But in a picture on glass there is no grain, at least no visible grain, and when thrown on a screen by a good lantern, it can be viewed by a number of people at one and the same time. The amateur photographer will find no end of pleasing occupation in translating his negatives into this form. Still more pleasure will he find in describing his rambles to his friends, accompanying his remarks, by first-rate pictorial illustrations.

HOW TO ENLARGE SMALL PHOTOGRAPHS.

The amatuer photographer who on the score of expense or because of its greater portability elects to purchase a small camera rather than a large one, will always have the satisfaction of reflecting that his small pictures can be enlarged. The image afforded by the camera is so perfect in its details that (unless this enlargement be carried to an extravagant extent) it suffers no harm by being greatly magnified. As a proof of this we may point to the ordinary photographic lantern slide, the visible part of which measures less than three inches in diameter. Yet such tiny pictures are constantly used by professional lecturers, who think nothing of showing them enlarged by the limelight on a screen measuring 15 to 18 feet across. We give this as an instance of the perfection of detail which a good photograph is capable of affording. The amateur will be content if he can enlage his quarter plates, or 5 × 4 negatives to 12 × 10 or 15 × 12. We would not advise him to attempt any larger size than the latter, at any rate, until he has had some experience of this branch of photographic work.

Before proceeding to enlarge a negative the operator must consider one important point. Does he want one or two copies of the enlarged picture, or does he require a dozen or more ? In the first case he will seek to produce enlarged positives direct on paper. In the latter case his best plan will be to obtain an enlarged negative from which as many prints can be obtained as he may require by the ordinary method with the printing frame. The negative may be a paper one if preferred, for paper admirably adapted to this purpose can now be obtained.

There are many different methods by which an enlarged picture can be obtained. Many of these require an extensive plant such as amateur workers would never think of purchasing. A few years ago such work would not be attempted except by experienced professional photographers, but since the introduction, about five years back, of a special kind of paper called "gelatino-bromide" paper, the operation of enlarging has been so much simplified that it now presents no great difficulty. The paper mentioned is in every respect similar to a gelatine plate, except that the sensitive emulsion of bromide of silver, instead of being supported on glass, is spread upon paper. It is sold in light tight boxes, at a cheap rate, and in dealing with it all the precautions against access of white light which are necessary in working gelatine plates must be observed.

The simplest and cheapest method of enlarging is to use daylight as the illuminator, and the following method may be recommended. Choose a window, if possible, from which there is an uninterrupted view of the sky. Carefully close it all up with brown paper, except a space sufficiently large to contain a printing frame holding the negative to be enlarged. The frame must be without its back and with the springs removed from it. The negative can be supported in it by tacks, and the film side should be placed inwards towards the room. This frame can be easily supported in position at a convenient height by strips of wood, one above and one below, screwed at each end into the window frame. To the lower strip also attach a shelf large enough to hold a camera. The camera is placed on this shelf with its lens pointing away from the window.

Having arranged these details, it will be found that an enlarged image of the negative will be cast upon a sheet of cardboard held a few feet from the camera, the size of the picture depending upon the distance. By moving the camera to and fro on its shelf, which should be long enough to give a little play in this respect, the image can easily be sharply focussed.

Now place on a table a box or board which can act as a solid screen for the reception of the image. It must be firm, whatever else it be. Cover it with white paper or tack a sheet of cardboard upon it. This is your focussing screen. Mark out upon it a space 15 × 12, or any other size that you may determine upon, and move it and the camera until the image fills the space. Take a strip of the gelatino bromide paper, 2 or 3 inches wide and 12 inches long, and after covering the negative in the window with a piece of card so as to shut off the light, pin this strip to your screen. Place in front of it a piece of orange paper which will cover three-quarters of it, so that when you uncover the negative and allow the light to do its work only one-quarter of the paper strip will be affected. Now expose for, say 5 minutes. Cover the negative, and uncover another quarter of the strip, and expose once more for 5 minutes. Do this the third time with another quarter, and once more with the whole strip exposed to the light coming through the negative. As a result you have a trial strip of paper the four parts of which have received exposures respectively of 5, 10, 15, and 20 minutes. Develope this strip, and it will be an unfailing guide to the amount of density obtainable with a negative of a certain quality and under certain conditions of light. The experiment may seem a tedious one, but it is worth the trouble, and will perhaps save many a sheet of sensitive paper which would otherwise be sacrificed in trial exposures.

As to development, we need not describe it here, because copious directions accompany each packet of paper. We may merely remark that the method employed is the ferrous oxalate formula already given, but it is modified in one or two details.

Those who depend upon daylight, especially dwellers in London, or other large cities and towns, have many a day of disappointed hopes. But they need not despair, for enlargements can be taken during the dullest days, or at night by means of the apparatus shown at page 126. This is virtually a magic lantern with an extended front. It is fitted with a patent light, giving a wonderful amount of illumination.

The secret of getting the greatest efficiency from any illuminant, the electric light excepted, is to furnish it with plenty of oxygen. Pure oxygen is out of the question, unless we are prepared to undertake all the trouble involved in using a lime light. But as ordinary air consists one-fifth of the gas, and as it can be had free of cost, it answers every purpose. To increase the flame of the fire the housemaid uses a pair of bellows. By the same law a conflagration becomes more brilliant in a high wind. Applying the same principle to the lantern (and it may be a lantern for exhibition purposes, or an enlarging lantern) the inventor of this special form of lamp employs a fan worked by clockwork in the body of the lantern itself. This fan delivers a constant and regular supply of fresh air, which plays in and around the wicks, adding much to the brilliancy of the light, and at the same time acting as a ventilator, and keeping the lantern cool. The increase of light power is enormous, and as it is a firmly established law, that the size of a picture shown by a lantern is only limited by the amount of illumination available, this increase is of the very first importance. The clockwork which drives the fan requires winding up once or twice during an evenings work with the instrument, an operation as noiseless and easy as the winding of a watch. This application of an old principle to the lantern is entirely new.

In using the enlarging apparatus with this artificial light, the front lens is used as an objective, and casts the enlarged image on a wall or screen. Upon this screen is fixed the sensitve paper, and the light given is so great that a quarter plate negative can be enlarged to 15 × 12 in about 3 minutes.

APPARATUS FOR PHOTO-MICROGRAPHY.

Workers with the Microscope are generally desirous of obtaining pictorial records of many of the objects whose structure that wonderful instrument allows them to examine. Hitherto such records have been made with the pencil, by the aid of an attachment to the Microscope, known as the Camera lucida. But although the artist may be conscientious as well as skilful, it is next to impossible for him to obtain a really trustworthy representation of what he tries to copy. This is because a draughtsman cannot help investing his work with a certain individuality; so that although two men might try their best to faithfully copy the same object, the results would show a very great amount of dissimilarity. We all know that a man's handwriting is something peculiar to him, and that its particular traits will become evident even if he tries to write in a feigned manner. So it is with an artist's pencil, a circumstance which enables experts to detect the work of different known hands with unfailing accuracy.

Now it is evident that in the pourtrayal of Microscopic objects, where truth is the one thing needful, and where artistic touches are not required; the photographic plate can give a more correct result than any mere drawing. This is now conceded by the best workers, and Photo-Micrography as it is called, has become a branch of science in which many excel. With these preliminary remarks, we will proceed to give such detailed directions as will enable those who are desirous of doing so, to succeed in this very interesting and instructive field of photographic work.

First of all, let us say a few words with regard to the type of Microscope to be employed. It need not be an expensive one; but it is advisable that it should possess a circular revolving stage having mechanical adjustments for centreing the object. It must be firm, and on some description of foot which cannot readily be knocked over. It must be so constructed that the entire instrument with the exception of the foot can be bent down to the horizontal position. Its tube should be short and thick. It must have a coarse adjustment, regulated by rack and pinion in the usual way, and also a fine adjustment. This latter should be so conveniently placed on the instrument, and its milled head cut with a groove, that it can be turned by means of an attached cord, in the manner to be presently described. The stage upon which the objects are placed, should be a revolving one, with brass clips to hold the slide firmly in position when the instrument is placed horizontally. Beneath the stage there should be an internal screw to receive a condenser. And it may be mentioned here that an achromatic object glass of the triple (French) form answers the purpose well. But care should be taken that the power of this condenser should never exceed the power of the objective in use. The French triplet, consisting of three glasses, each mounted separately, but screwing together, admits of regulation in this respect. For instance, in using the quarter inch objective, two of the French ones would be employed. But if the eighth objective were in use, then the complete triplet would form a suitable sub-stage condenser. With the inch power no condensing lens on the sub-stage would be necessary.

The ordinary lens of the camera is removed, and a short tube (lined with black velvet, and of such a diameter that the microscope tube will easily slide within it) is put in its place. The eyepiece of the microscope having been removed, the tube is slipped into the velvet lined aperture just described. The microscope tube should also be lined with velvet, or reflected light is sure to do some mischief when photography is commenced. The lamp is now placed behind the stage, as shown in page 128, and must be very carefully adjusted to the correct height. In front of it is placed the condenser, with its convex face towards the camera. A low power objective, say a one inch, is now screwed on to the microscope, the lamp is lighted, and the ground glass focussing screen of the camera examined. If every part of the apparatus has been correctly centred, the screen should exhibit a clear disc of light. If one portion appears to be brighter than another, it is quite certain that something is out of centre. The lamp may possibly be a little out of adjustment, or the condenser perhaps wants to be moved a trifle. A friendly assistant will be of great use here in trying the various adjustments while the operator, covered with the focussing cloth, is watching the screen. Until a clear disc is obtained, the work cannot proceed further.

When all seems to be perfect in the above respects, an object can be placed upon the stage and roughly focussed with the coarse adjustment. This object should be some well known one, so that the operator may know how it should appear, and what to look for. And now we must use the fine adjustment. It has been already pointed out that the milled head of this latter should be provided with a groove. In this groove is slipped a silk cord which is geared to a pulley wheel upon a long focussing rod at the side of the table (see page 128. The other end of this rod is furnished with a button which is within reach of, and can readily be turned by the hand of the operator as he watches the focussing screen.

In a photographic lens the visual and chemical foci are made to coincide, so that a picture which appears to be sharply defined on the camera screen will give a sharp picture when photographed. But in the microscope objective this is not always the case, and more especially in the case of low powers will this difference of foci become apparent. So that an image which appears to be sharp enough on the screen, turns out to be indistinct in the negative. Where this difficulty arises, it can be corrected in the following manner. After the image appears to be sharply defined, turn the fine adjustment so as to make the objective approach towards the object until the image on the focussing screen appears to be surrounded by a red areola. Although at this point it may not seem to be as sharply defined as before, the resulting negative will be all right.

After the lamp is lighted and all adjustments made, the apparatus may with advantage be allowed to rest for a short time, for the heat concentrated on the lenses, etc., is likely to cause slight expansion. The object can be focussed while the camera bellows is but extended one half. It can afterwards be extended until the image on the screen is of the desired size, and the fine adjustment brought into requisition as a finishing touch. The screen is now folded back, and the dark slide charged with its gelatine plate or plates is slipped into position. A blank card is placed against the sub-stage to shut off the light, the dark slide shutter is drawn, and now all is ready for taking the photograph. All that remains to be done is to remove the blank card for as long a time as may be judged necessary for exposure.

Upon this subject of exposure we can say but little, for it is governed, as in the case of an ordinary photograph, by a great many circumstances. One advantage however is possessed by the Microscopic worker, and that is that his source of light is a constant one. He is not dependent upon fickle daylight. (It may be mentioned here, that daylight or any other light except that proceeding from the lamp, must be rigorously excluded during all operations. But of course the red lamp may be kept burning with advantage, both as an illumination for the room, and for the necessary chemical work). But he will soon find out that length of exposure is governed in great measure by the nature of the object photographed. If the mounting medium (generally Canada balsam) be of a yellow tinge, this alone will necessitate greatly prolonged exposure. Then again, the object may be purposely stained with some nonactinic dye such as aniline brown. The best results will be obtained if the worker is clever enough to prepare his own slides. It would take us too far from our subject to go into this matter of mounting. But information upon the subject can be readily obtained from the various excellent books upon the Microscope now published. Of these we may mention Wood's "Common Objects for the Microscope," Davies "On Mounting Microscopic Objects," and the large treatises of Carpenter and Beale.

WEIGHTS AND MEASURES.

PHOTOGRAPHIC formulæ are compounded by Apothecaries' Weight. Dry chemicals are preferably weighed out in scales with glass pans. Liquid chemicals are measured in a graduated glass measure. Both measure and scale pans should be kept scrupulously clean.

APOTHECARIES WEIGHT.

DRY.

20 grains = 1 scruple.
3 scruples = 1 drachm = 60 grains.
8 drachms = 1 ounce = 480 ,,
12 ounces = 1 pound = 5760 ,,

WET.

60 minims = 1 fluid drachm.
8 drachms = 1 ounce.
20 ounces = 1 pint.
8 pints = 1 gallon.

It must be noted however, that the chemicals are sold by *Avoirdupois* Weight, in which the ounce and the drachm have other values.

AVOIRDUPOIS WEIGHT.

$27\frac{1}{3}$ grains = 1 drachm.
16 drachms = 1 ounce.
16 ounces = 1 pound.

Formulæ from foreign sources are generally compounded in grammes instead of grains. The following table for their conversion either way, will be found useful.

1 gramme	= 15·43	grains.
2 ,,	= 30·86	,,
3 ,,	= 46·29	,,
4 ,,	= 61·73	,,
5 ,,	= 77·16	,,
6 ,,	= 92·59	,,
7 ,,	= 108·03	,,
8 ,,	= 123·46	,,
9 ,,	= 138·89	,,

1 grain	= ·0648	grammes.
2 ,,	= ·1296	,,
3 ,,	= ·1944	,,
4 ,,	= ·2592	,,
5 ,,	= ·3240	,,
6 ,,	= ·3888	,,
7 ,,	= ·4536	,,
8 ,,	= ·5184	,,
9 ,,	= ·5832	,,

THE FOLLOWING ARTICLE

ON

EXPOSURE

IS KINDLY CONTRIBUTED

BY

A. S. PLATTS, Esq.

EXPOSURE.

To the beginner in Photography the question presents itself, "how long shall the cap remain off the lens during an exposure;" and, "what is the duration of the mystic period, known as 'correct exposure'?" So many varying elements enter into its composition, that it expands and contracts, grows and diminishes, and seems ever to elude the grasp of the panting neophyte. Correct exposure is the Will-o'-the-wisp of Photography. The many hued tints of changing nature, the bright-eyed sky, the sombre woodland, the stretching landscape, the solemn gloom of the cathedral aisle, the glamour of noon-day, the dying twilight, the sweet touch of spring, the golden richness of autumn, the cold shiver of winter, the tiny circlet that shields the glistening lens, the nervous sensitiveness of the quivering plate, all minister at the shrine of "correct exposure;" and all these the novice must conquer if he would ensnare thè wayward sprite.

That the factors of subject and lighting, time of day and year, aperture and plate, may be considered each in due course, and not left to haphazard conjecture or doubtful inspiration, I have laid down rules for my own guidance in the following tables, which the beginner may do well to follow :—

Before making an exposure, I find out by a glance at Table I. what is nearest the subject in hand. I write down the figure I decide upon, and multiply it by a figure from Table II.; I next multiply the product by a figure from Table III. which agrees with the stop I am using, and the product I divide by a figure from Table IV. agreeing with the plate I am using. The answer is in seconds, and is the length of exposure the subject requires.

TABLE I.—Subject and Light.

Compiled and slightly altered from Eder's and Burton's Tables.	Sunshine.	Diffused Light.	Dull.	Very Dull.	Gloomy
Sea and Sky	¼				
Panoramic View	1	2	3	4	5
Do. with Thick Foliage, or strong foreground, or light buildings	2	4	6	8	10
Dark Buildings	3	6	9	12	15
Heavy Foliage Foreground ...	4	8	12	16	20
Woods and badly lit River Banks	10	20	30	40	50
Living objects outdoors	4	8	12	20	30
Portrait near window	8	16	24	40	60
Interiors ....upwards of	100				
Copying same size	6	12	20		

TABLE II.—Time (Dr. J. A. Scott).

HOUR OF DAY a.m.	p.m.	JUNE.	MAY. JULY.	APRIL. AUG.	MARCH. SEP.	FEB. OCT.	JAN. NOV.	DEC.
12		1	1	1¼	1½	2	3½	4
11	1	1	1	1⅓	1½	2⅓	4	5
10	2	1	1	1¼	1¾	3	5	6
9	3	1	1¼	1½	2	4	12	16
8	4	1½	1½	2	3	10		
7	5	2	2½	3	6			
6	6	2½	3	6		Yellow Sunset affects these figures.		
5	7	5	6					
4	8	12						

TABLE III.—Lens and Stops.

U. S. Stops.	Intensity Ratio Stops.	Exposure.
4·	F 8	⅔
6·25	F 10 Unit	1
8·	F 11·31	1¼
9·	F 12	1½
12·25	F 14	2
16·	F 16	2½
20·25	F 18	3[illegible]
25·	F 20	4
32·	F 22·62	5
36·	F 24	5¾
42·25	F 26	6¾
49·	F 28	7¾
56·25	F 30	9
64·	F 32	10¼
81·	F 36	13
100·	F 40	16
128·	F 46·25	20½
144·	F 48	23
182·25	F 54	29
225·	F 60	36
256·	F 64	41
306·25	F 70	49
400·	F 80	64
512·	F 90·50	82
576·	F 96	92

TABLE IV.—Plates.

Unit.—Very Slow Plate, Panoramic View in Sunshine, June Noon, F 10 Stop, 1 Second Exposure.

Sensitometer Numbers.	Divide by
10	2 to 4
11	3 ,, 5
12	3 ,, 5
13	4 ,, 6
14	4 ,, 8
15	5 ,, 10
16	6 ,, 13
17	8 ,, 16
18	10 ,, 20
19	12 ,, 25
20	15 ,, 28
21	20 ,, 35
22	25 ,, 40
23	30 ,, 45
24	35 ,, 50
25	40 ,, 60
Unknown	10 ,, 30

NOTES TO TABLES.—Table I. This table must be used intelligently. A panoramic view I take to be a stretch of country with nothing particularly prominent in it. If masses of thick foliage are present (not in foreground) I double the exposure, but this must be done with judgment, varying this and every other item as I think the subject demands. No rule of thumb adherence must be given to this table. Thus I photograph my friends in diffused light in open air, but in such a secluded built up spot, that I always set down 16 or double the table to commence with.

In copying it must be remembered that if, as invariably occurs, the focus is lengthened, longer exposure must be given. Thus I copy a print same size in diffused light with my W.A. lense of 6 inch focus.

To focus correctly, I must lengthen to 12 inches, which means 4 times extra exposure. Four times 12 (copying in diffused light) are 48, that is 48 times exposure of a view in sunshine. When focus is lengthened, ascertain the relative exposures by squaring the two numbers, and divide the greater by the lesser. Thus as above, $6 \times 6 = 36$, $12 \times 12 = 144$. Divide latter by former; answer 4, that is, the 12 inch focus requires 4 times exposure of the 6 inches. By the same rule a portrait near window (about $1\frac{1}{2}$ feet distance, camera outside window) requires longer exposure for every foot or distance from window, thus a given light at 1 foot distance will be 4 times weaker at 2 feet, 9 at 3 feet, 16 at 4 ft., &c. As however so much depends on size of window, and whether it has open view of the sky or not, together with distance from it, that I have refrained from giving a figure for "portrait in ordinary room."

Table II. This requires no comment, beyond giving all the credit for its compilation to Dr. J. A. Scott, of Dublin.

Table III. If the beginner knows the focus of his lens and the numbers of his stops, the table is ready to his hand. If not, however, it is imperative that he shall find them out. The length of focus is ascertained by measuring the distance betwixt the focussing screen, and the object glass of a single lens, or the diaphragms (stops) of a doublet lens. Focus sharply on some distant object, and measure accordingly. Next measure *accurately* the diameter of each stop aperture. Divide the length of focus by this diameter, and if the answer is—say 28, the stop is called F28. Thus 10 inch focus with 1 inch diameter of stop would be F10. If the student desires to use the Uniform System Numbers (column 1), he must ignore column 3, and multiply by the figures in column 1. It is necessary however at the same time to use figures $6\frac{1}{4}$ times greater in Table IV. The Uniform System unit is F4.

Table IV. If the sensitometer number of plate is known, divide by a medium figure between the two given in column 2, and alter until the figure best suitable for the developer in use, and the exposure most desired (full or severely correct) is arrived at. In using an unknown plate the same plan must be adopted. Let it be understood that lower figures mean longer exposure, and *vice versa*. The plates I use myself for most work are of the cheapest, registering 18 sensitometer, and I divide according to subject with 15 to 20.

EXAMPLE OF EXPOSURE.—Suppose a village scene in diffused light at 3 p.m. in April, F30 stop, plate sensitometer 18. Table I. light buildings, &c., 4 multiplied by $1\frac{1}{2}$ (Table II.) = 6, multiplied by 9 (Table III.) = 54, divided by 15 (Table IV.) equals $3\frac{3}{5}$ seconds.

Diffused light, means bright sky without sun, or where no sun shines on subject. Dull—sky partially overcast. Very dull—much overcast. Half-points between any of these two may be used.

FILMS
AND
PAPER NEGATIVES.

PHOTO-
MECHANICAL
PRINTING
PROCESSES.

FILMS AND PAPER NEGATIVES.

THE introduction of films and paper as supports for the sensitive emulsion, whilst it was received with acclamation by amateurs, has after extended trial proved extremely disappointing. The advantages in favour of the new-comers are saving in weight, freedom from halation, and less chance of breakage; but the disadvantages of some extra trouble, some, and often, extremely prolonged operations, in addition to the usual ones of development and fixing, have and still out-weigh the above advantages. The writer has used every film and negative paper in the market, and has given them all a fair trial, but still adheres to the old standard dry-plate. Films are recommended, especially for those engaged in photo-mechanical or carbon printing, as they can be printed from either side, but as the same effect may be obtained by the use of the ordinary dry-plate, with no more trouble than is required for a film, the writer prefers even for this work to use the trusty and reliable glass support.

The first introduced was the negative paper, which, as its name implies, consisted of an emulsion upon an almost grainless paper, but it was found to be impossible to totally eradicate the grain, hence another support, such as a film of insoluble gelatine or a temporary support of paper was invented.

It is of course obvious that some mechanical method is required to strain the paper flat in the dark slide, or from the natural tendency of the paper to curl or bend up the picture would be out of focus. For this purpose an ingenious carrier has been devised, which is extremely simple and reasonable in price, but when on a tour it is of great convenience to be able to expose on as many subjects as one may desire without having resource to the dark room for the purpose of changing the films. They are therefore sent out in long bands of sensitive tissue on rollers, which by an ingenious arrangement can be exposed in successive portions till the whole is exposed. The arrangement by which these bands of emulsion can be manipulated is termed a roller slide, and whilst there are many such in the market, the writer has no hesitation in recommending as the simplest and the best that called the Optimus, which, unlike all others, requires no alteration of the focussing screen, but is simply inserted as an ordinary dark slide. It possesses also a special checking apparatus, which makes it impossible to wind off more than is required for one exposure, and also an automatic registering contrivance, which makes it absolutely self-chronicling, and impossible to cut the paper, except in the right place.

For developing the different kinds of films, the processes are precisely the same as for dry-plates, and the beginner may either use the method and the solutions for developing recommended at page 27, or he may employ the following which is perhaps an improvement:—

Pyro Solution.

Pyrogallol ... ... 480 grains.
Metabisulphite of Potash ... ... 480 „
Distilled water to make 15 ounces of solution.

Bromide or Restraining Solution.

Ammonium Bromide ... ... 480 grains.
Distilled water to make 4 ounces of solution.

Ammonia Accelerator.

Liq. Ammonia, 880 ... ... 1 ounce.
Distilled water ... ... 9 ounces.

FILMS AND PAPER NEGATIVES. 77

POTASH AND SODA ACCELERATOR.

Carbonate of Potash ... ... 480 grains.
  „   Soda 480   „
Ferrocyanide of Potash 480   „
Distilled water to make 10 ounces of solution.

Hydrokinone may also be used and is one of the best developers for a beginner, as it is practically free from stain, and gives much latitude of exposure ; or the Ferrous Oxalate Developer, recommended on page 28, may be used.

Hydrokinone or Quinol is one of the best developers for a beginner, as it is suitable alike for negative and positive work, and is practically free from the staining proclivities both of hands and film, so characteristic of Alkaline Pyro. It possesses also the great advantage of being especially a developer which will correct to a great extent any errors in exposure, as by the judicious use of this reducing agent, great over-exposure may be corrected and negatives of good printing density be obtained, and likewise for under-exposure it enables one to obtain a much better result than with Pyro, developing all possible detail, with no risk of fog if properly used; it is in this respect far superior to Pyro or Ferrous Oxalate. Full instructions are given on page 91.

As most of the commercial films and paper negatives differ slightly in their manipulation, a short *resume* of the process for each may be of some assistance.

EASTMAN'S STRIPPING FILM.

This consists of an insoluble sensitive film of gelatine emulsion attached temporarily to a paper support.

Immerse the film face downwards in a dish of clean cold water, taking care that no air bubbles adhere to it. When thoroughly limp, place face upwards in a developing dish, and pour on the developer, and proceed with development as recommended at page 27. When development is completed, rinse in two or three waters, and then fix in the following fixing-bath :—

    Hyposulphite of Soda ... ... 4 ounces.
    Water ... ... 16 ,,

It is absolutely necessary for film-work of any kind that no alum or any other chemical should be added to the fixing-bath. When thoroughly fixed, which will be in about ten or fifteen minutes, wash in the tank provided for that purpose, or by placing in a stream of running water. Leave it washing for half-an-hour, and clean a glass-plate, a little larger all round than the negative film, and coat it with the following solution :—

    Masticated India-rubber ... ... 10 grains.
    Benzole ... ... 1 ounce.

Allow it to dry for about five minutes, and then coat with enamel collodion, made as follows :—

    Pyroxylin ... ... 6 grains.
    Methylated Spirit ... ... ½-ounce.
    ,, Ether ... ... ½-ounce.

When the collodion has set, that is, when it will not drop from a corner of the plate, wash it thoroughly under the tap till the surface no longer repels water, or till the water runs off without any sign of greasiness ; now place the collodionised plate face upwards in a dish of cold water, bring the negative film into contact with it under the surface of the water, lift both out, and place film upwards on a pad of blotting-paper, lay a sheet of blotting-paper over it, and squeegee into close contact, using considerable pressure in all directions to wipe off superfluous water. Now place the film between sheets of blotting-paper for fifteen minutes, when it will be ready for the stripping process. For this operation, immerse the glass-plate bearing the film into a dish containing water at about 150 deg. to 200 deg. Fahr. temperature, rock the dish slightly, and the paper will be found to gradually float off ; it should be entirely removed, and all adherent portions of soluble gelatine removed by brushing with a camel's hair brush or tuft of cotton wool. Now wash the film in cold water. and immerse in the clearing bath of alum and citric acid recommended at page 29. After thoroughly washing in running water for about two hours the film is ready for transfer to its final support, for which purpose a special stripping skin is prepared, which must be soaked in water for two minutes, not longer; the film is brought in contact with it under water and squeeged into optical contact, and set aside to dry for four or five hours, after which period the edges may be trimmed with a knife, and the film easily stripped from the glass.

Solutions used in developing the film should not exceed a temperature of 75 deg. Fahr., and the fingers should only touch the films at the corners while wet. Printing from these films may be done from either side, but that which was in contact with the glass at the time of the transfer is the right one. Ground-glass placed in the printing frame with the ground-glass towards the negative will keep the film flat, and give very soft effects.

MORGAN AND KIDD'S NEGATIVE PAPER.

The paper is first soaked in water and then developed as above, well washed and placed in an alum bath,—composed of alum 2 oz., water 20 oz.,—for 5 or 10 minutes, well washed and then placed in a fixing bath. After thorougly washing again it can be placed in an alum and citric acid clearing bath and dried, which is best done by mounting it on collodionised glass, as described under Eastman's Film. It will be found that a further operation for making the paper transparent is required, and for this purpose vaseline or vaseline oil, which can be obtained from any chemist, snould be freely applied to the paper, and then the negative is left in a warm room for about 12 hours to allow the oil to soak into the pores of the paper. After the lapse of 12 hours excess may be wiped off by a tuft of cotton-wool or flannel. To store these oiled negatives they should be preserved between sheets of paper impregnated with stearine, which can be obtained from any chemist.

CELLULOID FILMS.

Notwithstanding the introduction of the above-mentioned films, manufacturers have been for some time in search of a support even more satisfactory which should require no stripping, and no extra processes. And at the commencement of this year (1889), films were introduced, made of celluloid. Their treatment differs practically in no way from glass plates, except that they should be allowed to soak in water for about thirty seconds prior to development, and with Quinol development, at least double that time. If the amateur has mastered the principles laid down in the previous chapter on development (pp. 18—39), he will have no difficulty in successfully developing these films. After fixing and washing, a five minutes' immersion in the following bath will be found beneficial :—

Glycerine, ½oz.; water, 10oz.

After soaking, pass a tuft of cotton wool over the surface of film, to absorb adherent solution, and allow to dry by hanging up from one corner. When the surface is dry lay the film face down on clean paper, and clean the back of the film with a soft cloth, or pad of flannel.

PRINTING FROM THE NEGATIVE
BY THE FERRO-PRUSSIATE, BROMIDE, PLATINOTYPE AND CARBON PROCESSES.

On pages 32, 33, and 34, will be found complete directions for printing upon silver-albumenized paper, but here it is proposed to give concise directions for obtaining prints from a negative in other colours than those given by albumenized paper, such as blue, black, sepia, brown, red chalk and various shades of purple and black.

FERRO-PRUSSIATE OR BLUE PRINTS.

By this process bright-blue prints on a white ground are obtained, and although not pleasing to all they afford an agreeable relief to the monotone of albumen prints, and it is especially suitable for sea-scapes. It is also the easiest of all printing processes, easier even than that with silver paper, as when the print is taken no operation of toning is required. The paper can be bought very cheap, and of a bright yellowish green colour; it will keep almost indefinitely, if kept perfectly free from light and damp. The paper should be cut to the required size and placed in the printing frame with the coloured size next to the negative; the back being placed in position the frame is exposed to light; and the print examined from time to time till it is seen that the whole of the detail is visible in an olive bluish green shade. The paper should now be removed from the frame and washed in water or under a tap, when it will be seen that the image will turn bright-blue and the ground of the paper turn white,—the paper should be washed till the drippings from it are quite colourless. Should the paper from having been improperly kept or overprinted show a bluish tinge in the whites, it can be dipped in a bath of ammonia,—one drachm to the half-pint of water — and then after rinsing once in a bath of hydrochloric acid of the same strength, the print should be allowed to dry, when it can be mounted in the ordinary way.

BROMIDE PAPER.

By means of this, prints can be obtained more quickly than by any other process, but there is more trouble as the image is invisible till developed. The paper is coated with an emulsion the same as a dry plate, and is, therefore, equally as sensitive to light, and great care must be exercised to conduct all the operations in the dark room. When properly manipulated it yields prints of a fine engraving black colour without any gloss. The paper is placed in the printing frame with the sensitized surface next to the negative; some beginners find a difficulty in telling which is the sensitized surface, but there should be no such difficulty from the appearance, but if there is, the piece of paper should be laid on the palm of the hand for a moment when the sensitized surface will curl inwards. The back of printing frame being placed in position, the paper is then exposed to daylight for two or three seconds, or, preferably, to gaslight or lamplight, as more control is obtained over exposure; hold the frame about three feet off the gas-burner for 10, 20, or 30 seconds according to the density of negative, and for 30 or 40 seconds to lamplight. Experience alone can determine the duration of exposure. The paper is removed from the frame in the dark room, and placed in the developing dish, and water poured on it till the paper is thoroughly limp, the water being then poured off. The developer, Ferrous Oxalate. recommended on page 28, may be used; or the following is perhaps an improvement :—

No. 1.

Neutral Oxalate of Potash ... 1440 grains.
Distilled Water ... ... 12 ounces.

PRINTING FROM THE NEGATIVE. 83

No. 2.

Ferrous Sulphate... ... ... 540 grains.
Sulphurous Acid ... ... 3 drops.
Distilled Water ... ... 4 ounces.

Add one part of No. 3 to seven parts of No. 1, and add

Sulphurous Acid ... ... 1 drachm,

and two or three drops of Bromide of Potash solution (page 26). Pour the developer evenly on the paper, and the image will soon begin to start into view. When the whole of the detail is visible, and the print is black enough, it is plunged immediately, without washing, into a clearing bath of

Acetic, Hydrochloric or Sulphuric Acid 1 drachm,
Water ... ... 5 ounces,

and allowed to remain for five minutes, and then into another bath of the same strength for the same time and then into a third. It should be then washed in water for 10 minutes, and fixed in a hypo bath of about four ounces to the pint, for about 15 minutes and then allowed to dry. Bromide Paper, as a rule, is sent out in three grades :— (*a*) smooth surface, thin paper, most suitable for mounting ; (*b*) smooth surface, thick paper, for book illustrations, and (*c*) rough surface thick paper, most suitable for enlargements of portraits and portraits by contract printing described above.

ALPHA PAPER.

This is somewhat similar to Bromide Paper, but yields prints more resembling albumenized prints by a little manipulation in exposing and developing. The paper may be exposed in the ordinary printing frame to diffused daylight from one to twenty seconds, according to the actinic power of the light and density of the negative. It may also be exposed to gas or lamp light, and the printing frame should be placed at about six inches from the flame, and an exposure varying from thirty seconds to five minutes, will be found necessary. The process of development employed is usually the ferrous oxalate, recommended on pp. 28 and 83. The prints may be either soaked in water first, or placed in the dry state in the developer; if the latter plan is adopted it will be found that they will have a tendency to curl, but this may be avoided by laying the print face downwards for a second or two on the developer, and then turning them over, and immersing bodily in the developer. After development, the prints must be plunged at once into the following clearing solution, for one or two minutes:—

Alum	1 ounce.
Citric Acid	¼ ounce.
Water...	20 ounces.

After five minutes washing in several changes of water they may be placed in the following toning bath:—

Hypo...	2½ ounces.
Sodium Acetate	½ ounce.
Sulphocyanide Ammonium ...	4 ounces.
Chloride of Gold	4 grains.
Distilled water	10 ounces.

Dissolve the ingredients in the order given.

The prints should be left in this bath till on looking through them the desired tone is obtained, then wash in running water for at least an hour, and hang up to dry; if an enamelled surface is desired they may be treated in the same way as recommended for gelatino-chloride prints (page 89).

The following general hints to ensure success and regularity of tone, will be found useful:—

Always use a good yellow light for the dark room illuminant when working this paper. Always use artificial light to expose by. Always place the printing-frame in exactly the same position; and give absolutely the same exposure to prints from the same negative. Clean hands are a *sine quâ non*. Hypo should never be touched till all the prints are developed. Do not over-develope, as the prints lose nothing in toning and fixing. If the prints are too dense, a longer soaking in the alum bath will reduce them. Always keep prints on the move in all solutions. In hot weather immerse the prints in an alum bath (1 ounce of alum to 10 ounces of water) after they have been well washed on leaving the fixing and toning bath. Over-exposure is known by a poor, flat print full of half tone, but wanting in contrast and vigour in the shadows. Under-exposure, known by want of half tone and greenish tints in the shadows.

Alpha Paper like Bromide may be developed with Hydrokinone (for formulæ see page 94), and gives very fine black tones by this method of development. It must, however, be well washed before being put into the clearing solution after development.

If the tone of the finished print, by either method of development, be unsatisfactory, it may be easily remedied by immersing the print, which if dry should be previously soaked in water until wet, in the Mercuric Chloride solution, page 29, till bleached, more or less, then washing thoroughly and redeveloping with Hydrokinone or Ferrous Oxalate ; it must be remembered, however, that this is a process of intensification, and, therefore care must be exercised not to carry the bleaching and redevelopment too far, so as to block up the details. The print should then be placed in the ordinary fixing bath for five minutes, and thoroughly well washed.

PLATINOTYPE PAPER.

By this, prints are obtained of a fine black colour by development, the image being formed by metallic Platinum, one of the most permanent metals known ; the results are extremely pleasing and very permanent. The paper is sent out by the Platinotype Company in tin tubes, so as to preserve it from damp which is a sure destroyer of it. It is printed in the printing frame in the ordinary way, but the image is only partially visible, but it prints in about one-third the time of ordinary albumenized paper. When printed deep enough it is developed upon a solution of neutral Oxalate of Potash, 130 grains to the ounce heated to a temperature of 150° to 170° Fahr. The print is placed face downward on the solution for 5 or 6 seconds, and is then placed immediately in a bath of hydrochloric acid (1 to 60), and after being moved about in this for ten minutes it is treated in the same way in two successive similar baths for like periods. The print is then thoroughly washed and pinned or hung up to dry and mounted in the ordinary way. For further directions the copious and complete directions issued with the paper must be referred to.

THE COLD PROCESS.

A modification of the above process has been introduced, in which, paper-coated with an iron salt, ferric oxalate, is exposed under a negative, till the image is distinctly visible, and it is then developed upon a mixed solution of oxalate and chloro-platinite of potash. In the hot process the platinum and iron salt are applied to the paper, but in this the platinum is deposited on the paper from the developer.

It is claimed for this paper by Mr. Willis, of the Platinotype Company, the inventor, that several advantages accrue from the use of this process, viz., greater transparency in the shadows, tentative and cold development, shorter exposure, and easy variation in the tone of the resulting print. For full details the beginner is referred to the instructions issued by the above company. The question as to which is the best process depends solely upon the amount of work to be done, few prints and occasional are best treated by the hot process, as in this case the cold process is rather more expensive, but where much work is required the cold process should be adopted.

Printing-out Platinotype Paper.

A process invented by Captain Pizzighelli is one well worth attention by any amateur. Paper-coated with a mixture of Ferric, and Alkaline Oxalate, and a salt of Platinum, with some organic matter, such as gum or starch, is exposed under a negative in the ordinary way, and when the image shows distinctly, the paper is either steamed by means of a kettle, or breathed upon when the image starts up into a permanent and pleasing black, formed by the reduction of the Platinum salt. Full directions will be found in the instructions as issued by the makers.

Carbon Process.

One of the earliest and certainly in results the most pleasing of all processes for the production of prints, which can be produced in almost any colour and upon any material, the only objection being, that negatives which are reversed as regards left and right must be used unless what is called double transfer is used, or one of the film negatives. The full directions are so complete and numerous, that the amateur is referred to the Manual of Carbon Printing by the Autotype Company. The paper, or tissue, as it is called, is coated with a gelatine containing colouring matters, and is sensitized with bichromate of potash, exposed to light, the duration of exposure being timed by an actinometer. The paper is then temporarily affixed to a support and developed from the back with water at 110° Fahr., and the print soon shows in all its beauty, and is then fixed in cold water and alum, or is transferred to its final support. The paper is cheap and can be bought ready prepared, in which state it will keep for about a fortnight, and from the facility with which coloured prints are obtained, the process should find a place in every amateur's work.

Gelatino-Chloride or Chloride Emulsion Printing-Out Paper.

This paper which is made by precipitating Chloride of Silver in a solution of Gelatine so as to make what is technically called an emulsion, and coating paper with the same, will in many instances give much finer results than the ordinary sensitized printing paper, which is coated with salted albumen, and sensitized on a solution of Nitrate of Silver. From the character of the coating of the paper, it yields prints which possess much greater contrast and detail in the shadows, and is, for this reason, especially useful for thin or flat negatives wanting in these characteristics For those negatives possessing great contrast the ordinary albumenized paper will give better results. . The Gelatino-Chloride paper is printed in precisely the same manner as the ordinary paper, as directed on page 33; but the depth of colour should be rather deeper in the finished print as it loses somewhat more in toning and fixing. Care must be exercised as this paper is rather more liable to become discoloured and stained. The prints require a slightly different method of toning, and the following may be considered as the best process to adopt. The prints must be thoroughly well washed in several changes of water, and then soaked in solution of alum (1 in 20) for five minutes, and again washed and transferred to one of the following baths:—

I.

Chloride of Gold	3 grains.
Potassium Sulphocyanide	36 ,,
Hyposulphite of Soda	1½ ,,
Distilled Water	12 ounces.

This gives purplish-brown tones of great beauty and richness of colour.

II.

a.

Acetate of Soda	1 ounce.
Chloride of Gold	10 grains.
Distilled Water	25 ounces.

b.

Ammonium Sulphocyanide ...	120 grains.
Chloride of Gold	5 ,,
Distilled Water	10 ounces.

These solutions will keep well separately; and for use must be mixed in the proportion of 3 ounces of *b* to 10 ounces of *a*. This also gives good purplish tones.

III.

a.

Ammonium Sulphocyanide ...	½ ounce.
Alum	½ ,,
Ammonium Carbonate	2 grains.
Distilled Water	25 ounces.

b.

Chloride of Gold	3 grains.
Distilled Water	20 ounces.

Mix by pouring 3 parts of *b* into 4 parts of *a* stirring constantly. This gives fine chestnut-brown tones, free from any bluish tint. If used more concentrated it will give blacker tones.

IV.

Combined Toning and Fixing Bath.

Hypo	6 ounces.
Sulphocyanide of Potash	1 ,,
Acetate of Soda	1½ ,,
Alum	96 grains.
Distilled Water	21 ounces.

Fill the bottle containing this solution with scraps and clippings of spoilt prints, or add 100 grains of Chloride of Silver, and leave for twenty-four hours, and add

Chloride of Gold ... ... 15 grains.
Chloride of Ammonium ... ... 30 „
Distilled Water ... ... 6 ounces.

When placed in this bath the prints turn bright yellow, and run through the scale of colours to a brilliant purplish-black. The preliminary alum bath is not required.

V.

Hypo... ... ... 3 ounces.
Chloride of Gold ... ... 6 grains.
Lead Nitrate ... ... 3 grains.
Distilled Water ... ... 20 ounces.

The prints should be placed in this without being washed previously.

After toning, the prints should be washed once in clean water, and passed into the following

Fixing Bath.

Hypo ... ... 1 ounce.
Water ... ... 10 „

and allowed to remain for at least five minutes, and then washed thoroughly with frequent changes of water for at least an hour.

GENERAL MAXIMS.

All toning baths should be mixed at least twelve hours before being used. The tone of the prints must be judged by holding them up to the light and looking through them. Extreme care must be exercised that greasy or hypo-contaminated fingers do not touch the prints. If the prints refuse to tone in well-defined spots, grease or hypo must be suspected; if in irregular patches with ill-defined outlines, the prints must be soaked in the alum bath for a longer period. If the edges turn greyish-blue or blue before the body of the print, the toning bath is too strong and more water must be added.

Prints on Gelatino-Chloride Paper may be treated in exactly the same way as ordinary albumen prints, but they should be trimmed before becoming quite dry, and mounted with fresh starch paste or gelatine, or by means of the indiarubber solution (page 78). When mounted, the face of the prints should be gently rubbed with a clean, moist wash-leather. Blotting paper must not be used. A very high gloss may be obtained by the following process :—

A perfectly clean piece of glass, preferably of patent plate, a cutting glass answers well, quarter of an inch larger all round than the print to be dried should be selected, and in the centre of this pour a small pool of the following solution:—

Yellow Resin ... ... 36 grains.
Yellow Wax ... ... 12 ,,
Turpentine or Ether ... ... 2 ounces.

Rub this all over the plate with a tuft of cotton wool till dry, and then polish with a clean piece of wool. Immerse the print and glass into a dish of cold water, and bring the print face downwards on to the waxed glass; raise from the water, and by aid of a squeegee, bring both into intimate contact; raise the glass bearing the print, and examine through the glass for any air bubbles, which may now be easily detected; if any are visible a piece of clean dry paper or indiarubber cloth should be placed over the print, and the squeegee again used till no bubbles are seen. Sheet vulcanite may also be used, or that known as Ferrotype Plates, these require no waxing until they have been used for some time. Rear the glass bearing the print on end to dry, and when thoroughly dry one corner may be raised from the glass with a penknife and the print easily stripped from its support. To mount these prints they should receive before thoroughly drying a good coating of fresh stiff paste, and the cards should be damped and the prints applied; but it must be understood that the print is stripped before being mounted. If there is any difficulty in stripping a print it should be placed for a few seconds before the fire, when they will generally leave their support of their own accord. Matt or dead surface prints may be obtained by treating ground glass with the wax solution and treating as described above.

HYDROQUINONE OR QUINOL DEVELOPMENT.

In the chapter on Development (pp. 18-31), full instructions have been given for the processes of Alkaline Pyro and Ferrous Oxalate development, but latterly Hydroquinone or Quinol has come to the front as a reducing agent. It is met with in commerce in grey or buff crystals, or brilliant needles of a slightly greenish-yellow hue: it is soluble in water about 1 in 30 more soluble in alcohol and glycerine. When exposed to the air it soon absorbs oxygen darkening in colour, and when kept in solution in water darkens also to a deep reddish-brown. It is closely allied to Pyrogallol or Pyro in chemical composition. To Captain Abney belongs the credit of having first introduced this re agent to the photographic world, and for some time it was considered but a curiosity, and was from its high price prohibited from coming into general use. Numerous experiments, however, and a great reduction in price, led to its being more generally used. At first the results were extremely disappointing, because the best method of using it was not known; with ammonia as an accelerator but poor results were obtained; but with the carbonates of potash and soda better results were given, but its action was extremely slow, development often being prolonged thirty or forty minutes. But when the Alkaline Hydrates were used, its value was at once recognised and it now holds a place almost if not equal to Pyro. It is essentially a beginner's developer as it allows great latitude of exposure, and may

94 HYDROQUINONE OR QUINOL DEVELOPMENT.

be used for any and every brand of plate or film, and is likewise useful for Bromide and Alpha Papers and Lantern Slides. The following formulæ are given as typical of the innumerable developers recommended. The first is the one we use personally, and is the one we have found, after numerous experiments, to be the most satisfactory for negative work :—

Stock Solution of Quinol.

Quinol ... ... 150 grains.
Sodium Sulphite ... ... 150 „
Sulphurous Acid ... ... 15 minims.
Distilled Water to make 10 ounces of solution.

Stock Accelerator.

Sodium Carbonate (pure) ... 1,300 grains.
Potassium Hydrate (Caustic Potash in sticks) ... ... 150 „
Distilled Water to make 10 ounces of solution.

For use, mix equal parts and dilute with twice or three times the quantity of water. One drachm of each with six drachms of water will be found sufficient for a quarter-plate which has received a normal exposure. If the plate has been over-exposed, or where over-exposure is known to exist, about $\frac{1}{8}$ grain of Bromide of Potassium, or one drop of the Bromide Restrainer (p. 76) should be added. For under-exposure, dilute with twice the quantity of water, or soak the plate first in the diluted accelerator, and then add the Hydroquinone solution after a minute or two.

Dr. Herklots Vos strongly recommends the following, which will be found a good formula also :—

Solution 1.

Quinol ... ... 4 grains
Sodium Sulphite ... ... 24 „
Distilled Water ... ... 1 ounce

Solution 2.
Potassium Bromide ... ... 60 grains.
Distilled Water to make 10 drachms of solution.

Solution 3.
Potassium Hydrate ... ... 2 ounces.
Distilled Water ... ... 1 ,,

For normal exposure add five drops of No. 2 and No. 3 solutions to one ounce of No. 1 and allow development to continue for some few minutes, then add another portion of No. 3 to obtain the required density. For under-exposure reduce the quantity of No. 2 solution to two drops, and gradually increase the accelerator No. 3 ; for over-exposure increase No. 2 to ten drops to the ounce. The above quantities are for a quarter-plate. The following is that recommended by a well-known firm of plate makers:—

No. I.
Quinol ... ... 160 grains.
Sodium Sulphite ... ... 2 ounces.
Citric Acid ... ... 60 grains.
Potassium Bromide ... ... 30 ,,
Distilled Water ... ... 20 ounces.

No. II.
Sodium Hydrate ... ... 160 grains.
Distilled Water ... ... 20 ounces.

For use mix equal parts of each.

The above formulæ will be found all that can be desired for negative work; but for positives, either on paper or on glass as transparencies, the following will be found very effective for black tones:—

Stock Solution I.
Quinol ... ... 120 grains.
Sodium Sulphite ... ... 360 ,,
Sulphurous Acid ... ... 18 minims.
Distilled Water to make 8 ounces.

HYDROQUINONE OR QUINOL DEVELOPMENT.

Stock Solution II.

Sodium Carbonate	...	...	960 grains.
Potassium Hydrate	...	...	120 ,,
Potassium Bromide	...	...	16 ,,

Distilled Water to make 8 ounces.

Mix in equal parts, and dilute with three times the quantity of water. The following will give a good purple tone to transparencies on glass, and brownish-fawn to Bromide paper :—

Quinol	...	...	...	...	2 grains
Ammonium Carbonate	...	...	24 ,,
Ammonium Bromide	...	...	$\frac{1}{4}$,,
Distilled Water	...	...	...	1 ounce.

Mix immediately before using.

In using Quinol as a developer there are one or two general principles which should not be lost sight of. Absolutely clean dishes must be used; any dish which has been used for pyro is unsuitable, and will stain the negative. The best results in negative work are obtained by using fresh developer for each plate, but the old developer need not be thrown away but may be placed in a separate bottle and use l for over-exposed plates. For positive work, fresh developer for every plate or print is not so much a necessity, an old developer working well for three or more plates. Negatives and positives should be well washed after developing and prior to fixing. The Hypo or Fixing Bath should not be allowed to get very discoloured or stains will ensue. And lastly, all plates whether negative or positive, should be cleared by the clearing solution recommended on page 29.

DETECTIVE OR HAND CAMERAS.

DURING the last twelve months a subject which has attracted much attention, is the use of detective or hand cameras ; which may be defined as apparatus, by means of which photographs may be taken without the knowledge of the general public. It is in such work as the taking of street views, marine pictures and photographs of rapidly-moving objects, and in the capture of the natural pose and expression of the unconscious human subjects, that the value of the hand camera is felt, as by its unobtrusive appearance, and the absence of all the somewhat tedious usual preparations which too often attract attention and destroy all natural charm, and give rise to that stiffness and self-consciousness which with most people seem to be the natural concomitant of "having their likeness took."

One of the earliest of this class of camera was the Book-shaped Camera," which notwithstanding many later introductions, can still hold its own for simplicity and effectiveness ; but now something a little more elaboate has been called for, as the use of this class of camera has been much extended, so as to include general all-round work. It would be impossible within reasonable limits to review in detail the great number which have been introduced to public notice, but a short consideration of the principal features of the various working parts will enable anyone to become at once a better judge of the practical efficiency of any instrument.

THE LENS.

The best form is undoubtedly that of the Rapid Euryscope. This working, as it does, at an aperture approximately one-sixth of its focal length, or f/6, renders it invaluable for extremely brief exposures. The next most suitable lens is the Rapid Rectilinear, which works with an effective aperture of f/8 ; then the Rapid View of the same aperture; and lastly the Wide Angle Euryscope working at f/9.50. It is essential that the lens besides being rapid, should possess that quality called depth of focus, or ability to define upon one plane, objects at varying distances from the lens, and as this quality decreases with an increase of focal length, lenses of comparatively short focus are used.

THE SHUTTER.

This should be capable of adjustment from a very rapid to a comparatively slow exposure. The speed at which the shutter should work will depend to a great extent upon the nearness and rapidity of movement of the objects in the field of view—not much assistance can be given on this point, experience alone will enable the worker to decide this.

DIAPHRAGMS OR STOPS.

Many operators assume that the use of a Diaphragm or Stop is not only unnecessary, but an evil when using a shutter at high speed; this, however, is a fallacy Except for dull days and for subjects with very heavy shadows, such as street views, &c., the open aperture of the lens is rarely necessary ; very fine work may and can be done with f/10, f/11 and even f/16 ; for beach or marine work, in brilliant sunshine, the latter is the largest aperture which should be used.

FOCUSSING.

Many hand cameras, especially those which have some automatic plate-changing arrangement, are not fitted with any focussing screen ; but we do not think this at all a desirable omission, and would be sufficient for us at least to reject the same, as our idea of the perfection of a hand camera is one which may be used for either work, that is, instantaneous or the ordinary time exposures with a stand. With lenses of short focus, focussing is not an absolute necessity, as there is always a point beyond which everything is sharp when the lens is racked out to its equivalent focus, and this may be easily found by experiment, or the following table will be of assistance, as showing approximately the nearest point in focus, with a doublet lens of given focus and aperture—

Focus.	f/6.	f/8	f/11	f/16.
4ins.	11ft.	9ft.	6ft.	4ft.
4½ins.	14 ,,	11 ,,	9 ,,	6 ,,
5ins.	19 ,,	14 ,,	11 ,,	8 ,,
5½ins.	21 ,,	16 ,,	12 ,,	9 ,,
6ins.	24 ,,	17 ,,	14 ,,	10 ,,

With a Rapid View lens of 5in. focus, anything beyond about 15ft. will be in focus with f/10 or f/11, with f/8 about 20ft.

DARK SLIDES, ROLLER SLIDES, CHANGING BOXES.

The question as to which of these three appliances is the best is purely a personal equation, as the decision will rest on the purpose for which the camera is desired, and the predilection of the owner ; as should he have a penchant for films, then a roller slide will become a necessity. The question as to dark slides or an automatic-changing arrangement will depend to some extent for decision upon the work for which the camera is intended. If for detective or hand work alone, then the absence of a focussing screen, which is the necessary feature of these cameras is not so much felt. And again another advantage of using dark slides is that one is not bound to use one particular brand or rapidity of plate, as many different kinds as holders may thus be tried, and the plate adapted to the special work in hand selected.

FINDERS.

No matter what the opinion of some few may be, we consider at least one if not two Finders an absolute necessity, as nothing is more annoying than to make sure that you have included the whole of some particular scene or object upon your sensitive plate, and then to find upon development that, notwithstanding your conviction upon this point, only half or part of the desired object is to be seen. The writer worked for some months without a Finder till, on a particular occasion, the much-desired object was conspicuous by its absence in one, and by being cut in half in another plate, both of which had been fired off on a certain occasion, the like of which would not occur again for twelve months. After that he mounted two Finders. Should any doubt exist as to their function, their usefulness will at once be appreciated when the explanation is given that a Finder shows in miniature, and not reversed, the subject thrown upon the sensitive surface by the lens; thus in the case of photographing any moving object, such as a yacht, the right moment, when the vessel is in the centre of the plate, may be seen, and the exposure made.

Having thus briefly considered the essentials for a hand camera, it only remains for us to give one or two general hints which may be of service. First, as to the plates to be used for ordinary instantaneous work, we undoubtedly recommend the most rapid that can be obtained, those marking 24 or 25 on Warnerke's Sensitometer; but at the same time one or two plates of a lower degree of rapidity should also be carried for time exposures. Secondly, as to the size, the most convenient will be found the quarter-plate or $4\frac{1}{4}$ by $3\frac{1}{4}$ ins., as from this size lantern slides may easily be made by contact printing, or they lend themselves equally well for the purpose of enlargement. Thirdly, as to the development of the plates. Rapid plates are most difficult of all to develope successfully, even when they have received time exposure of from $\frac{1}{4}$sec. and upwards, but when only the fractional part of a second, such as $\frac{1}{100}$, $\frac{1}{50}$ and so on have been given, then the successful development is a feat to be proud of. The method we strongly recommend is to soak the plate first of all in the alkali or accelerator, either ammonia p. 21; soda, p. 77; or potash, p. 27; then add after about one minute's soaking, $\frac{1}{4}$ grain of pyro or hydroquinone, and allow all detail to appear, then add more pyro or hydroquinone to allow the required density to be gained; in fact a very good plan, which originated we believe in America, is to soak the plate first of all in the accelerator and then transfer to the pyro or hydroquinone, allowing only the accelerator absorbed by the film to enter the second bath. This will usually be found sufficient, but if not, a slight addition of alkali to the pyro or hydroquinone will give the required density.

The Detective or hand camera shown in p. 113 is one which will be found to answer most effectively every requirement of the practical worker in this branch. A neat black leather covered box, $9\frac{1}{4}$ by $5\frac{1}{2}$ by $7\frac{1}{2}$ins., unsuspicious in character, encloses a camera, with space for six double-dark slides (three only being sent out with the camera), a sectional view of the same is given in p. 113; the other diagram gives a general idea of the external appearance and likewise gives the arrangements of its working parts. A sliding panel covers the lens when not in use, and an Euryscope, Rapid Rectilinear, or Rapid View Lens is supplied according to the length of the purchaser's purse. The shutter is so arranged that time or instaneous exposures may be given, the fastest being about the $\frac{1}{100}$ sec. The diaphragms are inserted in the lens tube in the usual manner upon opening the lid of the box. The dark slides are of specially light form, and the shutters pull right out, and the slides being much cheaper than the ordinary ones, allow more to be obtained without inordinate outlay. Two Finders are also fitted, which show the subject included on the plate when it is either vertical or horizontal; and a screw hole in the base enables it to be used upon a stand if desired.

PHOTO-MECHANICAL PRINTING PROCESSES.

So far this manual has treated of the production of negatives by photography, rather for the purpose of amusement than for any large commercial project, but it must not be supposed that the province of photography ends there. It is almost universal in its applications and the valuable aid which it renders to science, literature, and art. The illustrations for many of our serial illustrated magazines are in many cases effected almost entirely through the agency of the camera, and the processes by which these re-productions are made are termed Photo-mechanical, because photography in conjunction with a mechanical printing process is used. It would be impossible to enter at any length into minutiæ and working details of the different processes, but the following short resumé may give a general idea of the whole subject. Every process is founded upon the chemical action which light sets up in a mixture of gelatine and an alkaline salt of chromium. The precise chemical action is practically immaterial, but its results most important; its effect is to render the gelatine acted upon by light insoluble and incapable of absorbing water. The various processes may be divided into four classes :—

1.—Typographic Blocks, which are blocks, the groundwork of which is eaten away by some acid liquid, leaving the image in relief or raised up like any ordinary type; these blocks are chiefly used for illustrating serial papers.

2.—Plates in which the image is bitten, by the use of an acid liquid, leaving the groundwork untouched; the image is said to be etched in intaglio.

3.—Woodburytype, in which the image is on a very

thick gelatine film which is used to obtain a mould or impression on metal

4.—Collotype or Heliotype, in which the film itself is printed from.

1.—Typographic Blocks:—To prepare these the subject to be re-produced is copied by the collodion process, and after development the resulting negative is strongly intensified till the image shows as bare glass upon an absolutely opaque background. A print is taken from this negative in the printing frame in the ordinary way, upon paper coated with chromated gelatine, and after exposure taken from the frame and given a thin coating of printing ink, and soaked in cold water, when it is found that the printing ink will leave the gelatine in those parts protected from the action of light and only adhere to the image. This gelatine print in greasy ink, is now placed face downwards upon a sheet of zinc and passed through a press, when the ink leaves the paper and adheres to the zinc. The image on the plate is then further charged with ink and then etched, special precautions being taken to prevent the lines of the image from being eaten away by the etching fluid; when etched deep enough, the plate is printed from in the ordinary way in an ordinary steam-press.

2.—Plates etched in Intaglio :—By this process some of the most beautiful pictures of the day are produced. A film of chromated gelatine is exposed under a positive in the printing frame and developed. As in the carbon process the result is a film of gelatine bearing a picture in which the blacks are represented by little elevations and the whites by depressions; this film may be attached to a copper-plate and etchings begun at once, or it may be covered with powdered graphite and a mould taken from it by electrolysis. The plate when finished has to have the ink rubbed into the depressions representing the image, and the surface of the plate thoroughly cleaned between each impression taken from it.

3.—Woodburytype :—A film of chromated gelatine is exposed under a negative as usual, and cemented face downwards on to a sheet of glass, and washed for some hours under hot water; allowed to dry and stripped. It has at this period the apperance of an extremely thin transparent piece of silk, with the picture slightly in relief. It is then placed on a sheet of hard rolled lead and a plate of steel placed above it, and a pressure varying from one to five hundred tons brought to bear on it. The gelatine film is forced into the lead and makes an impression the same as a seal on hot sealing wax, the film itself being unharmed and ready to make any number of such moulds. The lead with the impression on it is now put into a press and special hot liquid gelatine ink is poured on to it, and a sheet of paper laid on top; pressure is brought to bear upon it, and the ink leaves the parts where there is no impression, collecting in the depression. The ink is allowed to get cold and the paper stripped, bearing the image with it; it is then washed in alum and dried.

4.—Collotype :—The most simple of all the processes. A film of chromated gelatine fastened to a glass or metal plate, is exposed under a reversed negative, washed and dried; only a very faint image can be seen at this point. The plate is now put in a press and damped with water and printer's ink applied with a roller, when it is found that the ink will adhere to those parts acted upon by light; the shadows in the picture will take most ink, the whites none. Paper is placed on the inked film and both passed through the lithographic press, and the result is the finished print.

For further instructions in these photo-mechanical processes, the amateur is referred to Wilkinson's "Photo-Mechanical Printing."

E. J. W.

PERKEN, SON & RAYMENT'S
OPTICAL
AND
SCIENTIFIC INSTRUMENTS.

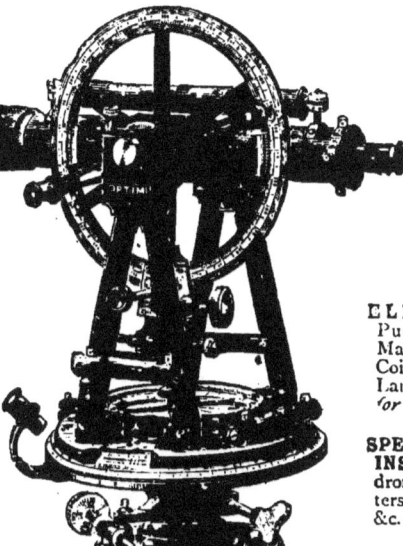

SPECTACLES, Eye Glasses, Folders, Hand Frames, Lenses either Spherical, Cylindrical, Sphero-Cylindrical, or Prismatic, White or Coloured Glasses of all Foci.

OPERA, Field, or Marine Glasses of every description.

TELESCOPES, Binocu'ar of Highest Power.

TELESCOPES, Monocular, Powerful.

MICROSCOPES, Microscopic Objects, Cabinets, Lamps, and all Accessories.

THERMOMETERS, Clinical, Chemical, Air, Sixes, Maximum and Minimum, &c., &c.

BAROMETERS, Mercurial, Board of Trade, Marine, Pit, & Household.

ANEROIDS Ships' Clocks, Sextants, Compasses.

MATHEMATICAL & SURVEYING INSTRUMENTS, Theodolites, Rules, Scales, T-Squares, Set Squares, Curves, Spirit Levels, Compasses.

ELECTRIC Bells, Pushes, Batteries, Magnetic Machines, Coils, Galvanometers, Lamps, Wire. *Agents for Gaiffe, Paris.*

SPECIFIC GRAVITY INSTRUMENTS, Hydrometers, Salinometers, Saccharometers, &c., &c

STEREOSCOPES, Graphoscopes, Praxinoscopes, Reading and other Magnifiers, Camera Obscura.

TRADE DISCOUNT LIST ON APPLICATION.

PERKEN, SON, & RAYMENT, 99, Hatton Garden, LONDON.

SPECTACLES, EYE GLASSES,
&c., &c.

Convex or Concave Glasses, blue steel spectacle frames, from 5s. to 42s. per doz.
„ „ Grooved Glasses, curl-side steel spectacle frames,
from 12s. to 42s. per doz.
„ „ Glasses, gold spectacle frames, per pair,
12s. 6d., 17s. 6d., 25s., 30s., 40s.
Double Eye glasses, (folding), steel frames, 9d. to 42s. per pair.
„ „ tortoise-shell frames, 12s. to 36s. per pair.
„ „ steel frames, grooved glasses,
12s. to 36s. per pair,
„ „ gold frames, 12s. 6d., 17s. 6d., 25s., 30s., 40s.
Single „ (Oxfords) 3s. to 9s. per doz.
Best Brazilian Pebbles to Spectacles or Eye Glasses, extra, Convex, 24s. to 100s
„ „ „ cut in the axe, extra, 42s. to 72s.
Coloured Spectacle Lenses of various tints, either concave, convex,
globular, or parallel.
Ladies' Hand Frames either of Tortoise-shell or Gold, inlaid or jewelled.
Cylindrical, Sphero-cylindrical Spectacles for cases of Astigmatism,
specially made to Oculist's formulæ.
Cases, for Oculists, containing Lenses for testing sight (spherical, cylin-
drical, prismatic) Trial Frames, Stenopaic Discs, &c., &c.

MAGNIFYING GLASSES FOR PICTURES, READING, &c.

Reading and Picture Magnifiers, in shell, ivory and metal, &c., 6d., 9d., 1s.,
1s. 6d., 2s. 6d., 3s. 6d., 5s., 10s., 12s. 6d., 15s.
„ „ „ (cylindrical), in shell ivory, metal, &c.,
7s. 6d., 10s. 6d., 15s., 20s., 30s. 40s.
High-power Magnifying Glasses for Botanists, in ebonite, shell, or metal
1s., 1s. 6d., 2s. 6d., 3s. 6d., 5s. 10s., 15s.

GRAPHOSCOPE, STEREOSCOPES, &c.

In Black Wood, ornamented with gold or painted flowers, 4s., 5s., 9s., 12s.
Grapho-Stereoscopes combined, 12s., 18s., 24s., 38s.
„ Walnut wood, superior, 5in. lens, 48s.; 6in., 60s.
Stereoscopes, 3s. 9d., 5s.; Achromatic, 13s., 15s., 19s., 30s. 40s.
„ on pedestal stands, 25s., 30s., 40s. 50s.
„ Revolving, for 50 slides, 60s.
„ „ 100 „ 130s.

PEDOMETERS.
£ s. d.
In Nickel-plated cases, registering to 12 miles 0 10 6
Ditto, Silver cases (Hall-marked) 1 0 0

TRADE DISCOUNT LIST ON APPLICATION.

PERKEN, SON, & RAYMENT, 99, Hatton Garden, LONDON.

OPERA, FIELD AND MARINE GLASSES.
OPERAS, Achromatic, in Cases.

	Diam. of Object-glass	1 1-8	1 5-16	1¼	1 5-8	1 7-8
	Morocco-cov'd bodies:	s. d.	s. d.	s. d.	s. d.	s. d.
	Japanned mounts...	6 9	7 3	9 0	11 6	13 3
	„ better qlty.	15 0	20 0	24 0	28 6	32 0
	„ 12 lens, supr.	21 9	27 0	32 0	36 9	42 0
	Ivory Bodies:					
	Gilt mounts... ...	14 6	18 0	23 0	27 0	42 0
	„ 12 lens, supr.	30 0	38 0	45 0	50 0	60 0
Pearl bodies:						
Gilt mounts	...	30 0	36 0	41 0	48 0	60 0
„ velvet cases, 12 lens, superior	...	57 6	66 0	95 0	120 0	150 0
Aluminium mounts, superior	...	48 0	60 0	68 0	77 0	90 0
Morocco or Russia	...	40 0	50 0	57 0	64 0	75 0
Pearl bodies	...	66 0	79 0	93 0	108 0	130 0
Tortoise-shell bodies	...	60 0	79 0	94 0	108 0	130 0
Inlaid Pearl, Ivory or Enamelled Bodies, very						
handsome, ...	superior	60 0	90 0	125 0	155 0	180 0

FIELD AND MARINE, Achromatic, in Sling Cases.

Diam. of Object-glass	1 3-8	1 5-8	1¾	2	2¼
Morocco bodies:	s. d.	s. d.	s. d.	s. d.	s. d.
Japanned mounts ...	15 0	18 0	24 0	28 6	34 0
„ „ better ...		32 0	35 0	38 6	41 0
Morocco or Russia, 12 lens,					
superior	40 0	44 0	50 0	56 0	60 0
Japan'd mnts., 12 lens, supr.	34 0	36 6	41 6	46 6	50 0
Aluminium, 12 lens, supr.	102 0	144 0	138 0	155 0	175 0

For 2-draw Field or Opera Glasses, add extra 10s to 30s.
For Bending Bar ditto to adjust centres, add extra 12s. 6d. to 34s.
Marine Glasses, specially adapted for night use, having large object-glasses and eye-pieces, 40s. to 50s.

BINOCULAR TELESCOPES.

Magnifying from 12 to 25 diameters, or 144 to 576 times. The definition will be found exceptionally fine. Arrangement for adjusting width between Eye-pieces.

		Diam. of Object-glass.		
Morocco or Russia bodies:	1 1-16	1 ⅝	1⅜	1¾
Japanned mounts, with	s. d.	s. d.	s. d.	s. d.
sun or spray shades ...	125 0	135 0	145 0	200 0
Aluminium mnts., shades ...	200 0	265 0	298 0	415 0
Morocco Conical bodies:				
Japanned mounts, no				
shades	84 0	92 0	100 0	...

The above prices include Sling Case.

TRADE DISCOUNT LIST ON APPLICATION.

PERKEN, SON, & RAYMENT, 99, Hatton Garden, LONDON.

'OPTIMUS' DWARF OPERA,
Leather Covered,
15/-

'OPTIMUS' GUINEA OPERA,
Morocco Covered,
21/-

'OPTIMUS' PEARL OPERA,
25/-

'OPTIMUS' ALUMINIUM OPERA.
50/-

'OPTIMUS' ECONOMIC FIELD GLASS.

Small Size ....
Clear Definition................ } **21/-**
Good Field of View Magnifying 16 times.............

'OPTIMUS' SCORER.

Is unrivalled for excellence and cheapness. It shows the number of people in boats four miles distant, Sea-birds one mile distant, and Bullet-marks on Target at 600 yards. } **30/-**
Magnifying 25 times.

'OPTIMUS' SCOUT.

Medium Size ......
Clear Definition ....
Good Field .... } **70/-**
High Magnifying Power (64 times).

'OPTIMUS' BINOCULAR OR DOUBLE TELESCOPE.

This Instrument has Bending Bar for Exact Visual Adjustment...
The Size is Moderate .... } **80/-**
The Definition is Crisp... ....
Very high (144 times) Magnifying

If with Shades, as Diagram ......} **100/-**

For General Excellence, Definition, and Magnifying Power, we invite intending Purchasers to test our Field and Opera Glasses against any in the world

Opera Glasses in great variety.

TRADE DISCOUNT LIST ON APPLICATION.

PERKEN, SON, & RAYMENT, 99, Hatton Garden, LONDON.

'OPTIMUS' TELESCOPES.

ACHROMATIC.

	Diameter of object glass	1in.	$1\frac{9}{16}$	$1\frac{7}{16}$	$1\frac{1}{4}$. 2
Morocco covered bodies—		s. d.	s. d.	s. d.	s. d. s. d
Brass mounts, 3 draws	... ...	5 9	8 0	15 0	21 0
,, and spray or sun shades		7 0	10 6	17 6	23 0
"Tourist" Morocco-covered bodies—					
Brass mounts, 3 draws and cap and sling	...	12 6	19 0	27 0	37 0
Oxidised mounts, 3 draws, cap and sun shades	15 6	23 0	30 0	41 0
	Diameter of object glass	$1\frac{1}{14}$	$1\frac{7}{16}$	$1\frac{3}{8}$	2	$2\frac{1}{4}$
"Army" Morocco-covered bodies—		s. d.	s. d.	s. d.	s. d.	s. d.
Oxidised mounts, 4 draws	... ...	31 0	41 0	58 0	72 0
"Navy" or "Day and Night" Morocco-covered bodies—					
1 draw, with shades ...	... ...	30 0	41 0	60 0	82 0
"Government," Morocco-covered bodies—					
Pancratic, 3 draws, with shades	... ...	42 0	54 0	72 0	90 0
"Yachtsman," Morocco-covered bodies—					
Tapered, 1 draw, with shades ...	... ...	34 0	42 0	57 0	77 0
"Rifleman's," Morocco-covered bodies—					
2 draws, exceptionally portable, but having high power	... ...	29 0	34 0	...	...
With still higher power	... ... ,..	...	40 0	...	...
"Deerstalker," Morocco-covered bodies—					
3 draws, cap and sling	... ...	26 6	...	44 0	58 0
"Viceroy," Morocco-covered bodies, 3 draws	...	25 0	...	40 0	55 0
"Empress," for ladies' use, being very light—					
Polished Aluminium bodies, covered with superior leather, 3 draws	...	80 0	95 0	...	130 0	...

Wood Tripod Stands for Telescopes, with gutter tops, adjustable, from 13s. to 30s.

ASTRONOMICAL.

	Diameter of object glass	$1\frac{1}{16}$	$1\frac{7}{16}$	$1\frac{1}{4}$	2
Portable, Morocco-covered, terres and celes		s. d.	s. d.	s. d.	s. d.
eye-pieces	... ...	9 0	18 0	23 0	36 0
,, on wood tripod stand for table, fitted in cabinet, complete	... ...	...	...	34 0	
	Diameter of object glass	$2\frac{1}{4}$	$2\frac{1}{2}$	$2\frac{3}{4}$	3 .
Brass body, best finish, rack motion for focussing, mounted on brass claw stand, vertical and horizontal adjustment, terrestrial and celestial	£ s.	£ s.	£ s.	£ s.
eye-pieces, fitted in cabinet, complete	...	9 0	10 5	14 0	16 10
	Diameter of object glass	3	$3\frac{3}{4}$	4	$4\frac{1}{4}$
Superior, as above, fitted with finder, rack steady-	£ s.	£ s.	£ s.	£ s.
ing rods, 2 terrestrial and 2 celestial eye-pieces, on best rigid stand, in cabinet, complete	...	30 0	35 0	54 0	70 0

TRADE DISCOUNT LIST ON APPLICATION.

PERKEN, SON, & RAYMENT, 99, Hatton Garden, LONDON.

'OPTIMUS' MICROSCOPES.

	£	s.	d.
Youth's, French made with single objective, in wood case	0	6	3
„ Superior, 11s. 3d., 15s. 9d., £1, £1 6s., £1 15s., £2 1s.,	3	2	0
Student's, English made, dividing objectives, giving 3 powers	3	6	6
„ Superior, with rack adjustment, with 2 eye-pieces — 2 objectives — condenser, &c., &c., £5 10s., £7 10s.,	10	0	0
University, dividing objective, giving 3 powers ...	3	3	0
Monocular, rack and pinion adjustment—glass stage, reflector, condenser, 2 eye-pieces—2in., 1in. and ½in. objectives	15	0	0
Monocular, as above, with Polarizing apparatus, 3 eye-pieces— 2in., 1in., ½in. and ¼in. objectives, double nose-piece...	22	10	0
„ Large size, circular revolving stage, graduated, milled heads to slow motion, suited for examining sections of crystals—3 eye-pieces, 2in., ½in., ¼in. and 1⁄10in. objectives	38	10	0
Binocular bodies, having the necessary additional eye-pieces suitable for the instrument ... extra from £4 to	9	0	0
Dissecting microscope, complete	2	10	0

Inches	4	3	2	1	1	⅔	½	¼	⅓	⅙	⅛	1⁄12	1⁄15
Microscopic Objectives ...	25	25	25	25	25		40	35	40	48	65		
Ditto, 1st quality— Angular aperture ...	9°	12°	16°	20°	27°	30°	80°	100°	100°	150°	140°	145°	150°
Greatest magnifying power ... diameters	72 20/6	112 40	140 40	196 46	280 46	420 50	620 77	1400 88	1480 105	1820 125/	2380 135/	5200 198/	6400 210

The first quality, half-inch and higher powers, are fitted with screw collar arrangement for adjusting distance according to thickness of covering glass.

	£	s.	d.		£	s.	d.
Polarising Apparatus ...	1	2	0	Section Cutting Machines from:	0	9	0
Parabola	0	16	0	Air Pump, with tray, &c. „	0	15	0
Spot Lens ...	0	8	0	Microscopic Object Boxes			
Double Nose-piece	0	12	6	1s. 4d., 2s., 2s. 6d.,			
Live Cage ...	0	3	0	3s. 6d., 4s.,	0	9	0
Stage Forceps ...	0	3	0	„ Object Cabinets,			
Camera Lucida	0	12	6	mahogany, 40s.	3	0	0
„ „ Wollaston's	1	4	0	„ Lamps, with Shades			
Lieberkuhn				6s., 10s. 6d., 14s.	1	0	0
Stand Condensers 5s. 9d., 7s. 6d., 15s.,	1	0	0	„ Dissecting Knives,			
Turn-table ... from	0	4	0	Scissors, Forceps, &c.			

All **Microscopic Accessories**, including objects (mounted and unmounted), supplied to order on the most reasonable terms.

TRADE DISCOUNT LIST ON APPLICATION.

PERKEN, SON, & RAYMENT, 99, Hatton Garden, LONDON.

'OPTIMUS' ANEROID BAROMETERS.

	s.	d.
Watch size, (1½ or 2 inch dial), Hard Enamel 26s. 6d.; Engraved Silvered	30	0
" with mountain scale, Enamelled 28s. 6d.; Engraved silvered 8,000 feet 33s.; 10,000 feet 36s.; 12,000 feet ...	42	0
" first quality compensated silvered dial	42	0
" first quality mountain scale silvered dial, 10,000ft. 50s.; 12,000ft. 54s.; 15,000ft. ...	65	0
Pocket size,(2½ or 3inch dial),compensated	48	0
Pocket size, with mountain scale, compensated, 10,000ft, 66s.; 15,000 feet, 75s.; 20,000 feet	83	0
Keyless motion for revolving altitude scale ... ... (extra)	8	0
Thermometers on dials ... ... "	3	0

Gold or Silver cases, hall-marked, extra according to weight.
Mining and Surveying Aneroid supplied to order.

ANEROIDS IN BRASS CIRCULAR MOUNTS and outside Boxes.

	Superior			Extra quality, with Thermometer		
	5-inch.	6	8	5	6	8
	s. d.	s. d.	s. d.	s. d.	s. d.	s. d.
Card Dials ...	12 6	22 6	36 0 ...	22 0	30 0	38 0
Enamelled Dials	22 0	29 0	44 0 ...	32 0	42 0	54 0
Silv'rd engraved	22 0	33 0	49 0 ...	32 0	42 0	58 0

£ s. d

Aneroids as above, fitted into carved oak and other wood cases, extra according to workmanship ... from 8s. 6d. to 5 0 0
Barograph by means of clock-work revolving drum carrying chart, the variations of atmospheric pressure are recorded ... 6 6 6
Kew verifications supplied with above instruments for a small extra charge.

MERCURIAL BAROMETERS.

	£	s.	d.
Fitzroy, in wood frames ... 9s. 6d., 12s. 6d., 20s.	1	5	0
Ditto Carved ... £1 10s.; £1 15s.; £2 8s.	3	2	0
Wheel pattern frames 6in. dial 18s.; 8in. 26s.; 10in.	1	18	0
Ditto, Superior ... 30s.; 8in. 48s.; 10in.	3	8	0
Pediment, in Oak, Rosewood, Walnut or Mahogany, Fig. 1, £1 4s., £1 16s., £2 18s., £4.	7	10	0
Marine Barometer with Sympiesometer vernier and gymbals, Fig. 2 ... ... £3 15s.	4	10	0
Standard Barometer ... £7 10s., £12 12s.	22	10	0
Board of Trade	3	10	0

FIG. 1   FIG. 2

TRADE DISCOUNT LIST ON APPLICATION,

PERKEN, SON, & RAYMENT, 99, Hatton Garden, LONDON.

MATHEMATICAL INSTRUMENTS.

	£ s. d.
Sets, French make, in wood boxes, complete, 1s., 1s. 3d., 1s. 9d., 3s., 6s., 10s.,	1 5 0
English, in Mahogany case, containing 6-in. electrum long-joint compass ink and pencil points and lengthening bar, ink and pencil bows, drawing pen, protractor, and ebony parallel ... each	1 10 0
Rosewood case, containing 6-inch electrum long-joint compass, ink and pencil points and lengthening bar, divider, ink and pencil bows, drawing pen, ivory protractor, and ebony parallel	2 2 0
Rosewood case, containing the following long-joint instruments:—6-inch compass with ink and pencil points and lengthening bar, divider, ink and pencil bows, set of three spring bows, two drawing pens, ivory protractor, and parallel	2 12 0

'OPTIMUS' THERMOMETERS.

	s. d.	s. d.
Clinical Indestructible, in boxwood or German silver cases ... ... 4 and 5 in.	3 0	6 in. 3 6
„ Indestructible Magnifying lens fronts ... ... 4 and 5 „	6 6	6 „ 7 6
Chemical, for immersion, 150°, 1s.; 220°, 1s. 6d.; 300°, 3s.; 400°, 4s.; 600°, 5s		

	8-inch s. d.	10-inch s. d.	12-inch s. d.
Fig. 1. Air, mounted on boxwood, spirit or mercury, enamelled tubes ...	0 5	1 0	2 0 Fig. 2.
„ superior, mounted on boxwood, spirit or mercury, enamelled tubes	1 6	2 6	3 6
„ Minimum, spirit, enamelled tubes	0 9	1 6	
„ Minimum, superior, spirit, enamelled tubes...	2 0	3 0	
„ Minimum, on porcelain, spirit	1 10	4 0	6 6
„ superior, on porcelain, spirit Fig. 1	5 0	6 6	8 0
„ Sixes, on boxwood	5 0	6 6	8 0
„ „ on porcelain or opal glass	9 0	11 0	12 9
Bath, or Brewer's, on metal scales, Fig. 2	1 0	1 6	2 6
Ditto, on porcelain scales, Forbes specifications		3 3	
Ditto, metal scales, copper cases ...	1 10	3 0	5 6

OPINIONS OF 'OPTIMUS' PHOTOGRAPHIC LENSES.

We now turn to the "Optimus Rapid Euryscope," manufactured by the firm of Perken, Son, and Rayment, Hatton Garden, an example of which is on a camera on our editorial table. With its full aperture of 1¾ in. (its equivalent focus being 11 in.) it defines with extreme brilliancy, and when used with a stop it easily covers a 10 by 8 plate to the corners, which is larger than that engraved on the mount as its possibility. Working as it does with such a large aperture ($f/6$ approx) it serves as a portrait and group Lens, as well as a landscape and copying objective. There is no doubt of its proving a most useful lens, J. TRAILL TAYLOR.—*British Journal of Photography.*

Frith's series of "Life in London Streets" were all taken with 12 × 10 *Portable* "OPTIMUS" lens on Cobb's plates. Had an "Optimus" *rapid* symmetrical been used, the plates would have been over-exposed with full aperture.—G. LINDSAY JOHNSON, M.A.,M.B., F.R.C.S., England.—*Amateur Photographer.*

PORTRAIT LENS.—The "Optimus" lenses are moderate in price, and yield most excellent results.—*Amateur Photographer.*

"OPTIMUS" LENS.—I have taken trains going at 30 miles an hour, and think the lenses perfect for rapidity and definition.—E. J. WALL.—*Amateur Photographer.*

. . . . We may call attention to the extensive optical and metal works that Perken, Son, and Rayment have established in Hatton Garden, and their photographic cabinet factory in Saffron Hill. At the former we were much interested in the glass-grinding departments—one for photographic lenses, another for spectacles : and we were surprised to find in London such extensive workshops for the metal parts of cameras and optical lanterns ; indeed, we thought outside Birmingham we should not find such workshops in the United Kingdom. The cabinet works in Saffron Hill also interested us much; the arrangement of the machine tools, and distribution of power on the several floors, being admirable.—*Photographic News.*

We are pleased to find upon trial that the Lens ["Optimus" Rapid Rectilinear] sent for review is really an excellent instrument.—*Photographic News.*

If E. G. E. wants the finest lens in the market he cannot do better than get the "OPTIMUS."—Professor DE FRERE.—*Amateur Photographer.*

"OPTIMUS EURYSCOPE."—I am much pleased with the 9 by 7 received last week. It covers 12 by 10, and gives splendid definition. For a good, useful, all-round lens I consider it perfect.—E. BRIGHTMAN, Hon. Sec., Bristol and West of England A. P. A.

"OPTIMUS EURYSCOPE."—When in your establishment you kindly lent me one of your 7 by 5 I like the lens so well, I do not want to part with it.—CHAPMAN JONES, F.I.C., F.C.S.

"OPTIMUS EURYSCOPE."—This lens is of extra large diameter ; the aperture being $f/6$, and while admitting of the most rapid exposures, gives fine marginal definition. We have obtained with it excellent portraits in an ordinary sitting room. The lens is a most useful one all-round.—T. C. HEPWORTH.—*The Camera*, April 1, 1889.

As I have often said before, I consider these lenses unequalled.—E. J. WALL, *Amateur Photographer.*

"I have tried the 7 × 5 'OPTIMUS' Euryscope. It is a very satisfactory lens and covers the *whole plate* for interiors with $f/16$; being able to work at $f/6$ makes it very handy for portraits."—J. G. P. VEREKER.

PERKEN, SON, & RAYMENT, 99, Hatton Garden, LONDON

IRIS DIAPHRAGM Fitted to Rapid Euryscope and „ Rectilinear	5 by 4 10/-	7 by 5 11/-	9 by 7 12/6	10 by 8 14/-	12 by 10 16/-	15 by 12 18/-	18 by 16 20/- Extra.

'OPTIMUS'
RAPID PHOTOGRAPHIC LENSES.

Extra Rapid Euryscope, large Diameter (Double). The aperture is F/6. The Lenses are of special optical glass, constructed with the nicest precision of curvatures, so maintaining good marginal definition, coupled with the most **Extreme Rapidity.**

To cover	5 by 4	6 by 5	7 by 5	8 by 5	9 by 7	10 by 8	12 by 10
Equiv. Focus	5¼	6¼	8¼	10	12	14	18 inches.
	63/-	78/-	94/6	110/-	126/-	220/-	380/-

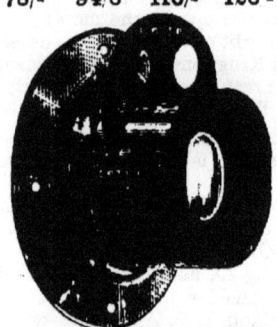

Wide Angle Euryscope (Double), F/9·50. This aperture is exceedingly open for wide angle work. The definition, however, is in no way sacrificed, as the curvatures are perfectly accurate, and the most minute detail in architectural and interior subjects is rendered with the maximum of crispness, and a total absence of distortion.

To cover	5 by 4	7 by 5	9 by 7	10 by 8	12 by 10
Equiv. Focus	4	4¾	6	8	10 inches.
	63/-	94/6	126/-	220/-	380/-

TRADE DISCOUNT LIST ON APPLICATION.

PERKEN, SON, & RAYMENT, 99, Hatton Garden, LONDON.

IRIS ·DIAPHRAGM Fitted to Rapid Euryscope and „ Rectilinear	5 by 4	7 by 5	9 by 7	10 by 8	12 by 10	15 by 12	18 by 16
	10/-	11/-	12/6	14/-	16/-	18/-	20/- Extra.

Portable Symmetrical (Double), F/16 with revolving diaphragms. Specially adapted for Architecture, being of short focus and wide angular aperture, can be used to advantage when very close to the subject. It is also useful for landscapes, as well as copying. The smaller sizes give beautiful **Lantern Slides,** the definition being exceptionally crisp.

To cover	$\tfrac{4}{8}$	$\tfrac{7}{8}$	$\tfrac{9}{5}$	$\tfrac{10}{8}$	$\tfrac{12}{10}$	$\tfrac{15}{12}$	$\tfrac{18}{16}$ plates.
	39/-	52/6	82/6	127/6	142/6	180/-	225/-

Rapid Rectilinear (Double) F/8.—Second only to the Euryscope for Rapidity therefore well suited for instantaneous effects, outdoor groups and views, as well as interiors. Copying and enlarging are also within the capabilities of the lens; in fact its work may be styled "**UNIVERSAL.**"

To Cover	$\tfrac{4}{4}$	$\tfrac{5}{4}$	$\tfrac{7}{5}$	$\tfrac{5}{8}$	$\tfrac{9}{7}$	$\tfrac{10}{8}$	$\tfrac{12}{10}$	$\tfrac{15}{12}$	$\tfrac{18}{16}$
Focus	5¼	6¾	8¾	10	12	14	18	20	25 inches
	33/-	45/-	49/6	64/-	82/6	127/6	142/6	180/-	225/-

. . . . We may call attention to the extensive optical and metal works that Perken, Son and Rayment have established in Hatton Garden, and their photographic·cabinet factory in Saffron Hill. At the former we were much interested in the glass-grinding departments—one for photographic lenses, another for spectacles; and we were surprised to find in London such extensive workshops for the metal parts of cameras and optical lanterns; indeed, we thought outside Birmingham we should not find such workshops in the United Kingdom.—*Photographic News.*

We are pleased to find upon trial that the Lens ["Optimus" Rapid Rectilinear] sent for review is really an excellent instrument.—*Photographic News.*

TRADE DISCOUNT LIST ON APPLICATION,

PERKEN, SON, & RAYMENT, 99, Hatton Garden, LONDON.

Rapid Landscape.—Works F/11, and gives brilliant negatives. Particularly suited for landscapes also capable of being worked as a Portrait lens.

To cover...	5 by 4	7 by 5	9 by 7	10 by 8	12 by 10 plates.
Focus ..	5¼	9	12	14	18 inches.
	25/-	36/-	45/-	75/-	110/-

Portrait Lens.—Specially constructed as quick acting for short exposures in Portraiture. They are second to none, the definition being maintained by their perfect optical qualities.

Diam.	2 inches.	2¾ inches.	3¼ inches.	
Price	90/-	120/-	180/-	*Larger Sizes to order.*
	1 B.	2 B.	3 B.	

'DEAR SIRS.—Herewith your 7 x 5 "Optimus' Lens, which, as per your request, I have tried in the production of large heads. Along with it I send two negatives taken by it, the head in one of them measuring *two* inches, that in the other being *three* inches. In both, the perspective seems right enough, there being no appearance of its being strained or violent.

'With us, it was rather dark and very rainy all day, and I took the negatives inside a room, without a diaphragm, exposure 7 secs. and 10 secs. respectively. The SHARPNESS of all the planes of the head is good, as you will perceive. The distance of the sitter from the lens was 3 ft. 0½ ins. for the larger head, and 4 feet 9 in. for the smaller head.—Yours truly, J. TRAILL TAYLOR.'

'If E. G. E. wants the FINEST LENS in the market he cannot do better than get the "OPTIMUS."—Professor DE FRERZ.'—*Amateur Photographer.*

TRADE DISCOUNT LIST ON APPLICATION.

PERKEN, SON, & RAYMENT, 99, Hatt·n Garden, LONDON.

"OPTIMUS" WIDE ANGLE CAMERA. EXTRA LONG FOCUS.

Baseboard does not cut off the view when using wide angle lenses

This Instrument possesses every possible advantage, being very Light, very Rigid, and very Portable. The focussing screen and body may be brought towards the front of Baseboard so as to prevent obstruction when using lenses of wide angular aperture and short focus. It is provided with double-swing arrangement and long-focussing (rack) adjustment. When closed the lens may remain attached to its proper position (the front), and project through the TURNTABLE Easeboard.

Price, including 3 Double Dark Slides—

4¼ by 3¼	5 by 4	6½ by 4¾	8½ by 6½	10 by 8	12 by 10	15 by 12
140/-	146/-	165/-	188/-	235/-	286/-	350/-

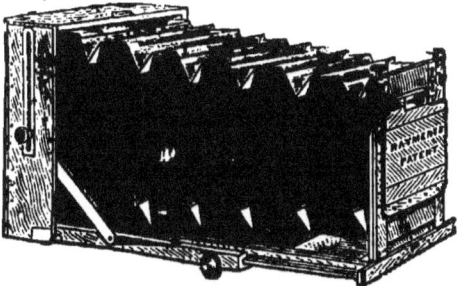

RAYMENT'S PATENT CAMERA. EXTRA LONG FOCUS.

"I should strongly recommend RAYMENT's Camera. It is LIGHT, COMPACT, very RIGID, and extends to about double the usual focus."—*Amateur Photographer.*

"The 'RAYMENT' Camera, in particular, claims attention. Both for its BEAUTY of WORKMANSHIP and for the EASE and READINESS with which it can be put into action."—*The Camera.*

It can be set up almost instantaneously, has no loose parts, and includes all motions having hinged focussing screen (adjusted by rack and pinion action), double swing back, cross fronts reversing back arrangement so that oblong dark slides give either horizontal or vertical pictures without unscrewing the Camera from the tripod.

Price of Camera, including 3 Double Dark Slides—

4¼ by 3¼	5 by 4	6½ by 4¾	8½ by 6½	10 by 8	12 by 10	15 by 12
12/-	126/-	145/-	168/-	212/-	258/-	31½/-

TRADE DISCOUNT LIST ON APPLICATION.

PERKEN, SON, & RAYMENT, 99, Hatton Garden, LONDON.

"OPTIMUS" CAMERA. LONG FOCUS

The Instrument can be set up almost instantaneously, has no loose parts, and includes all motions, having hinged focussing screen (adjusted by rack and pinion action), double swing back, cross fronts reversing back arrangement so that oblong dark slides give either horizontal or vertical pictures without unscrewing the Camera from the tripod.

Price of Camera, including 3 Double Dark Slides —

$4\frac{1}{4}$ by $3\frac{1}{4}$	5 by 4	$6\frac{1}{2}$ by $4\frac{3}{4}$	$8\frac{1}{2}$ by $6\frac{1}{2}$	10 by 8	12 by 10	15 by 12
130/-	133/-	137/-	175/-	227/-	275/-	333/-

"OPTIMUS" STUDIO CAMERA.

Specially arranged for Studio Use.

"Invited to say, if in our estimation, the Studio Cameras of Perken, Son, and Rayment could be improved in any way whatever, for the purpose for which they are intended, we must answer, No!" - *British Journal of Photography.*

This Camera is perfectly rigid, has double length of Bellows to suit small studios where large pictures are required, is fitted with Mechanical Adjustment to Focus, and swing back. It is in all respects a perfect Instrument.

Camera with repeating frame masks, and one single dark slide—

$6\frac{1}{2}$ by $6\frac{1}{2}$	$8\frac{1}{2}$ by $8\frac{1}{2}$	10 by 10	12 by 12	15 by 15
145/-	188/-	225/-	265/-	325/

TRADE DISCOUNT LIST ON APPLICATION.

"OPTIMUS" PORTABLE FOLDING CAMERA.

Cheap, Strong, Serviceable, and Efficient.

Durable bellows, hinged focussing screen with sliding adjustment, readily and securely held in exact position by means of a pinion passing through the body nearest bottom or baseboard and having milled head screws on either side of the instrument to clamp tight.

Camera and one Double Dark Slide—

4¼ by 3¼	5 by 4	6½ by 4¾	8½ by 6½
21/-	24/-	39/6	48/-

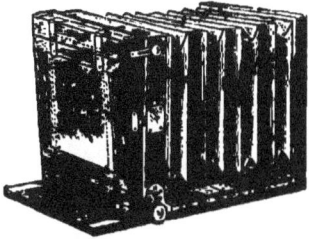

PORTABLE (A.R.) CAMERA.

Compact, Rigid, Inexpensive, and of Excellent Finish

These Instruments have Leather Bellows, and are fitted with hinged Focussing Screen, adjusted by Rack and Pinion, Square Reversing Back, so that horizontal or vertical pictures may be taken without removing Camera from Stand.

Price of Camera, including 3 Double Dark Slides—

4¼ by 3¼	5 by 4	6½ by 4¾	5½ by 6½	10 by 8	12 by 10	15 by 12
85/-	87/6	98/-	125/-	150/-	200/-	260/-

Extra for Brass Binding Camera, and 3 Double Dark Slides—

27/6	28/-	30/-	32/-	33/-	38/-	48/-

TRADE DISCOUNT LIST ON APPLICATION.

PERKEN, SON, & RAYMENT, 99, Hatton Garden, LONDON.

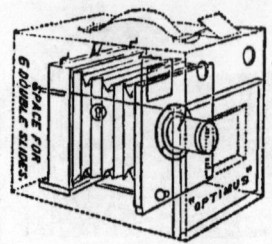

"OPTIMUS" DETECTIVE CAMERA.

Price, including three Double Dark Slides. £ s.
With Optimus Rapid View Lens Working F8 ... ... 5 10 0
Ditto, with "Optimus" Rapid Rectilinear working F8 ... ... 6 6 0
Ditto, with "Optimus" Rapid Euryscope working F6 ... ... 7 7 0
"Extra" Double Dark Slides each 8 6

The Shutter is arranged for exposures of any duration not less than $\frac{1}{100}$ of a second. The Shutter and Camera occupy so little space that six Double Dark-Slides, accommodating twelve Dry Plates, can be carried, in addition to a Focussing Screen. A panel slides up at the end of the box, displaying the screen for focussing. The exactness in focussing is simple, and the position is maintained by a secure clamping arrangement. A similar sliding panel is fitted to the front end, which completely hides the lens. The exterior is covered with leather, and measures 9¼ by 5½ by 7¼. (Negatives 4¼ by 3¼ or 8¼ by 3¼.)

Carries twelve dry plates.  Plates changed by turning a button.

"OPTIMUS" MAGAZINE CAMERA.
NO DARK SLIDES REQUIRED.

With Rapid Rectilinear Lens, working at F8 ... ... £6 6 0
With Rapid Euryscope working at F6 ... ... 7 7 0

Twelve dry plates are placed in the upper portion of the grooved travelling reservoir. The bases of these plates rest upon the top of the Camera body. The grooved reservoir recedes gradually from the Exposure Chamber when the pinion is revolved—allowing one plate at a time to fall to the bottom half of the reservoir, and so place its sensitized surface within the Exposure Chamber opposite to the Lens, and exactly in true focussing register. The rapidity and simplicity of working is unique. The twelve plates may, if desired, be exposed in as many seconds. There is no possibility of the plates sticking. The Shutter is suitable and convenient.

TRADE DISCOUNT LIST ON APPLICATION.

PERKEN, SON, & RAYMENT, 99, Hatton Garden, LONDON.

"OPTIMUS"
UBIQUE HAND CAMERA.
FOR PLATES 4¼ by 3¼
OUTSIDE DIMENSIONS OF CAMERA, 8 by 4½ by 6 INCHES.
This instrument has 3 Double Dark Slides and is self contained. The shutter ives rapid or slow exposures. With View Finder, Focussing Screen, and
"Optimus" Rapid View Lens, Complete 55/-
"Optimus" Rapid Rectilinear Lens, Complete 80/-

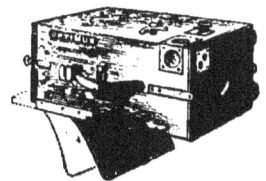

"OPTIMUS"
MINIMUS HAND CAMERA (PATENT)
FOR PLATES 4¼ by 8¼
OUTSIDE DIMENSIONS OF CAMERA 8 by 3½ by 5 INCHES.
This Camera has no Dark Slides, carries Twelve Dry Plates. . They place themselves consecutively before the Lens; each, after exposure, is removed to the back of the others by means of the little bag underneath the instrument. The register indicating the number of plate offered for exposure, renders it impossible for the same plate to be twice exposed. It is provided with Focussing Adjustment and View Finder, also with a Curtain Shutter which gives slow or rapid exposures.
Price with "Optimus" Rapid Euryscope £7 7 0

TRADE DISCOUNT LIST ON APPLICATION.

PERKEN, SON, & RAYMENT, 99, Hatton Garden, LONDON.

"OPTIMUS" (ECONOMIC, PORTABLE,) CAMERA (LONG FOCUS.)

STRONG, SERVICEABLE AND EFFICIENT.

It has long extension Taper Bellows, Rising Front, Rack Adjustment, Square Reversing Frame, and other modern improvements.

Price with Three Double Dark Slides—

4¼ by 3¼	6½ by 4¾	8½ by 6½
93/-	114/-	136/-

"OPTIMUS"
ECONOMIC PHOTOGRAPHIC SETS.

The above Camera is supplied with Dark Slide, Rapid Rectilinear Lens Instantaneous Shutter and Tripod, complete with waterproof case.

4¼ by 3¼	6½ by 4¾	8½ by 6½
84/-	110/-	160/-

TRADE DISCOUNT LIST ON APPLICATION.

PERKEN, SON, & RAYMENT, 99, Hatton Garden, LONDON.

"OPTIMUS"
PORTABLE SETS OF PHOTOGRAPHIC APPARATUS.

Fitted COMPLETE in Cabinet, with Tripod Stand.

	£	s.	d.
Quarter Plate Size (4¼ × 3¼) includes every requisite	1	16	0
Half Plate Size (6½ × 4¾)	3	10	0
Quarter Plate Size (4¼ × 3¼) as diagram	2	5	0
Half Plate Size (6 × 4¾)	5	0	0

Superior Camera, Rack and Pinion focussing adjustment,

		£	s.	d.
Quarter Plate	(4¼ × 3¼)	3	8	0
,, Half Plate	(6½ × 4¾)	5	15	0
,, Whole Plate	(8½ × 6½)	9	10	0

BRASS BINDING *any* CAMERA, and 3 Double Dark Slides—

4¼ by 3¼	5 by 4	6½ by 4¾	8½ by 6½	10 by 8	12 by 10	15 by 13
27 6	28 0	30 0	32 0	33 0	38 0	48 0

EXTRA DOUBLE DARK SLIDES for *any* of our Cameras—

	4¼ by 3¼	5 by 4	6½ by 4¾	8½ by 6½	10 by 8	12 by 10	15 by 12
Solid, no hinges— EACH	7/3	8/3	10/9	...	...	...	...
Solid, with hinged shutters EACH	10/3	10/9	11/9	...	...	...	...
Hinged opening and Hinged shutter EACH	14/-	14/6	15/-	21/6	25/6	31/6	47/3

TRADE DISCOUNT LIST ON APPLICATION.

PERKEN, SON, & RAYMENT, 99, Hatton Garden, LONDON.

CAMERA CASES, with Shoulder Straps,
LINED WITH GREEN CLOTH.

SQUARE— $\frac{1}{4}$, 20/-; $\frac{1}{2}$, 29/-; $\frac{1}{8}^0$, 35/-; $1\frac{2}{8}$, 46/- Leather.
$\frac{1}{4}$, 15/9; $\frac{1}{2}$, 20/-; $\frac{1}{8}^0$, 21.6; $1\frac{2}{8}$, 28/- Canvas.

OBLONG— $\frac{1}{4}$, 10/6; $\frac{1}{2}$, 15/-; $\frac{1}{1}$, 20/- Canvas only.

PORTABLE "UMBRELLA" RUBY TENT (PATENT
NON-ACTINIC.

Like an umbrella, it folds into a very small space, and can be set up for developing or changing plates as easily as its well-known prototype. Made of two thicknesses of material, one ruby, the other orange colour, no light can enter except it be filtered through these media. The head and hands are introduced so that the operator, sitting in his chair can conveniently watch the progress of his work whilst the tent rests on the table.—*Beginner's Guide to Photography.*

Made in two sizes—	Dimensions closed. Inches	Price s. d.
For changing Plates	24 by 3	25 0
For Developing ,, ...	28½ by 3	35 0

TRADE DISCOUNT LIST ON APPLICATION.

PERKEN, SON, & RAYMENT, 99, Hatton Garden, LONDON.

WAISTCOAT DETECTIVE CAMERA.

THIS INSTRUMENT IS ONLY MADE BY THE PATENTEE,
C. P. STIRN.

With Plates for 36 Exposures 23/6
" 24 " Larger }
Size for Lantern Pictures } 35/-

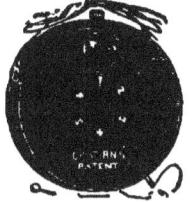

"OPTIMUS" VIEW FINDERS.

Camera Obscura Model ... ... each 5/-
1¼-inch bi-concave ... ... ,, 2/6
2¼ " " ... ... ,, 6/-
3¼ " " ... ... ,, 8/6

FOCUSSING GLASSES.

Per doz.—

9/9 · 15/9 18/3 33/9

With Archimedean Screw.

60/- per doz.

COMBINED FOCUSSING GLASS AND FINDER.

Bell Shape,   Screw Adjustment.   Sliding Adjustment
5/- each.   4/- each.   5/- each.

TRADE DISCOUNT LIST ON APPLICATION.

PERKEN SON, & RAYMENT, 99, Hatton Garden, LONDON

PATENT
PERFECTION PHOTOMETER.

CORRECT EXPOSURE A CERTAINTY.

Each ... 6/9.

"OPTIMUS"
MAGNESIUM
RIBBON LAMP, 5/-

British Journal of Photography, Nov. 7th, 1888 :—" It is a neat little thing, not greatly exceeding the dimensions of an old-fashioned watch, and projects a *powerful* beam of *light.*

HASTINGS'
FLASH LAMP.

1/3 With Mouthpiece. | With Pneumatic Ball **2/6**

" A handy Lamp. It is especially adapted for taking instantaneous photographs at night. The glass tube is charged with magnesium powder, and the brass trough filled with methylated spirit; this being lighted, the pneumatic ball is squeezed, the flash is given, and the photograph taken."—*Amateur Photographer.*

MAHOGANY
RETOUCHING DESKS.

Whole-plate	16/8
12 x 10	25/-
15 x 12	35/6

Each has the smaller Carriers.

TRADE DISCOUNT LIST ON APPLICATION.

PERKEN, SON, & RAYMENT, 99, Hatton Garden, LONDON

Magnesium Flash Lamp
FOR PHOTOGRAPHY.

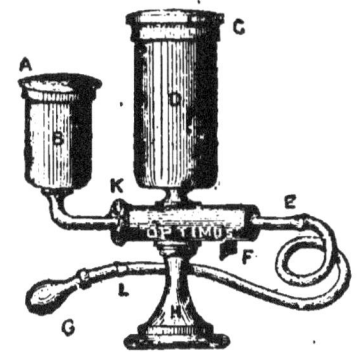

A Stopper of the Spirit Lamp.
B Spirit Reservoir.
C Stopper of the Magnesium Reservoir.
D Reservoir of Magnesium Powder.
E Junction of Rubber Tube.
F Spring Tap for conducting Powder to passage.
G Pneumatic Ball.
H Stand or Handle for supporting Lamp.
K Removable Screw Cap to allow Cleansing.
L Junction between Pneumatic Ball and Tube.

MODE OF USING THE LAMP.

Remove the Stopper **A** from the Reservoir **B**, fill the Reservoir **B** with as much spirit as the sponge will absorb, replace the Metallic Gauze as well as the stopper **A** to prevent evaporation.

Remove Stopper **C** from Reservoir **D**, into which pour the Magnesium powder, *which should be perfectly dry*. Replace the stopper **C** to prevent loss of Powder. The Lamp may be held in the hand or stood on a table or other support. The Lamp being now ready, remove the Stopper **A** and light the Spirit Reservoir, waiting until it burns well, press the Pneumatic Ball **G** to assure yourself that the air passes freely without extinguishing the flame. Press the Spring Tap **F** which will allow the Powder to enter the Tube above it and close again. Now on squeezing the Ball **G** the air will force the Powder through the flame and give a brilliant flash. By pressing the Tap **F** two or three times, more Powder can be burned, and a more intense flash may be obtained.

To create a continuous light remove the Pneumatic Ball **G** from the Rubber Tube at **L**, and blow softly with the mouth, at the same time holding open the Spring Tap **F** which will allow the Powder to enter the passage whilst the wind you blow into the Tube carries it through the flame.

The Screw Cap **K** may be removed to enable the passage to be cleansed, which is very necessary to the proper performance of the little machine.

PRICE ... *(Brass Nickeled)* ... **7/6 each.**

TRADE DISCOUNT LIST ON APPLICATION.

PERKEN, SON, & RAYMENT, 99, Hatton Garden, LONDON.

"OPTIMUS" PLUNGE SHUTTER (PATENT).

"Mr. J. Traill Taylor exhibited a pneumatic shutter, giving exposures of any duration, at will, and avoiding all vibration. He stated it was one of the best shutters he had seen, and said it was made by Perken, Son, and Rayment."—*British Journal of Photography.*

This may be styled the most **PORTABLE** of shutters. It is made either to fit on the hood, or may be adapted to act between the lenses of a doublet.

To fit $\frac{1}{4}$ or $\frac{1}{2}$ plate Optimus Lens	...	...	...	...	30/	Complete with Pneumatic Release.
,, $\frac{1}{1}$ ''	''	''	...	...	...	36/
,, 10 × 8	''	''	...	...	...	48/

"OPTIMUS" BETWEEN LENS SHUTTERS.

Is arranged to fit the lens mount like a saddle. Exposure is effected by a plunger working between the two combinations of a double lens, or in front of them if preferred. Both pneumatic and hand releases are provided. Exposures varying from $\frac{1}{75}$ of a second to prolonged may be attained. The working parts are strong, and derangement impossible with a reasonably careful operator. Weight and bulk are reduced to a minimum.

Prices same as above.

PHANTOM SHUTTER, with Hand Release.

For Diameter of Front Lens.

Inch.	$1\frac{1}{2}$	$1\frac{3}{4}$	2	$2\frac{1}{4}$	$2\frac{1}{2}$	$2\frac{3}{4}$	3	$3\frac{1}{4}$	$3\frac{1}{2}$
	13/-	14/6	15/9	16/9	18/3	19/6	20/9	21/9	23,3

IF FITTED WITH PNEUMATIC RELEASE.

	$1\frac{1}{2}$	$1\frac{3}{4}$	2	$2\frac{1}{4}$	$2\frac{1}{2}$	$2\frac{3}{4}$	3	$3\frac{1}{4}$	$3\frac{1}{2}$
	20/9	22/-	23,3	24/6	25/9	27/-	28 3	29/6	30/0

TRADE DISCOUNT LIST ON APPLICATION.

PERKEN, SON, & RAYMENT, 99, Hatton Garden, LONDON.

TRIPOD

AND

STUDIO.

"OPTIMUS" STANDS for CAMERAS.

	$\tfrac{1}{4}$		$\tfrac{1}{2}$		$\tfrac{3}{4}$		$\tfrac{10}{8}$	
	s.	d.	s.	d.	s.	d.	s.	d
Telescopic, with sliding leg adjustment, rigid	8	6	9	6	10	9	16	9
Folding Ash, with Bayonet joint, "E.P.," very rigid	9	9	10	9	12	6	20	3
Telescopic Ash, with sliding leg adjustment, "Maudsley" pattern	18	6	19	9	20	9	24	9
Telescope Ash, 3-fold, as sketch			22	0	24	0	29	0
'OPTIMUS' Stand, very rigid and much recommended for large sizes			15	0	16	0	22	6
*4-FOLD, Very Portable			20	0	25	0	35	0
Pine Studio Stands with clamp	14	6	30	0	RACK		43	9
Mahogany					45	0	78	9

* *Specially Portable. Strongly recommended where Small Bulk is important.*

TRADE DISCOUNT LIST ON APPLICATION.

PERKEN, SON, & RAYMENT, 99, Hatton Garden LONDON.

"OPTIMUS"
MICRO-PHOTOGRAPHIC APPARATUS.

	£ s d
Camera, with Dark Slide, Microscope, 2-inch Objective, Lamp, Condenser, &c.	9 10 0
Superior Camera and Microscope, with Rack and Pinion Adjustment Fitted for Focussing as well as for Adjusting the Stage... ...	14 0 0

HEAD RESTS.

Amateur, to fit on Chair ... 7/6

STUDIO

15/-   28/-   42/-

TRADE DISCOUNT LIST ON APPLICATION.

PERKEN, SON, & RAYMENT, 99, Hatton Garden, LONDON

OPTIMUS INFALLIBLE DEVELOPER.

THE Components of this Developer are perfectly pure, and the exact quantities necessary are employed, so ensuring the best possible negatives, whether Landscapes or Portraits, be the Exposures Instantaneous or Prolonged.

TO PREPARE THE DEVELOPER.

Place the contents of the three packets into a quart bottle and fill up with 40 ozs. pure (if possible distilled) water. When all is completely dissolved it is ready for use.

TO ECONOMISE THE DEVELOPER.

After developing, pour the used Developer into a second bottle, for it can be advantageously employed in developing other plates.

To obtain the best possible results we recommend the following instructions to the careful attention of the operator:

For Plates—
    Over Exposed ... ... use Old Developer only.
    Instantaneously Exposed ,, New Developer ,,
    Under Exposed ... ... ,, half old & half new.

Place the plate in the developing dish or tray and pour over it sufficient Developer to cover the upper surface thoroughly.

When the detail does not appear as quickly as expected add new Developer, or use new only, as may be found necessary.

IN PACKETS SUFFICIENT FOR 100 ¼-PLATES.
PRICE 1s. 6d.

TRADE DISCOUNT LIST ON APPLICATION.

PERKEN, SON, & RAYMENT, 99, Hatton Garden, LONDON.

DAYLIGHT DEVELOPING DISH.
PATENT.

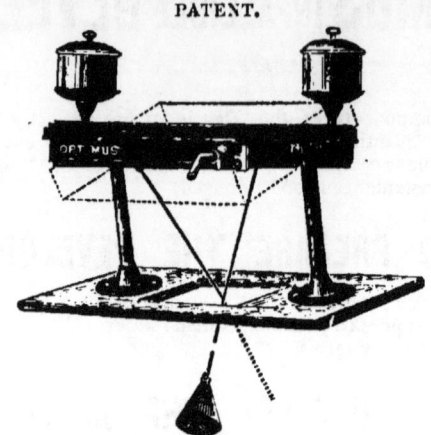

PERKEN, SON & RAYMENT, 99, Hatton Garden, LONDON.

WE would draw the attention of those who find the atmosphere and darkness of the dark room objectionable, to this apparatus which we have just completed, and which greatly reduces the time necessary for the operator to be imprisoned in the black hole—in fact, if a changing box or bag be used, the dark room is unnecessary.

It consists of a dish with non-actinic glass top and bottom, supported on a convenient stand, and having an **AUTOMATIC ROCKING ARRANGEMENT**, which keeps the dish oscillating during development.

At the sides of the dish external funnels communicate with the interior, and are so arranged that white light cannot reach the plate. Through these funnels solutions are conveyed to the plate within, which may be strengthened or weakened at will, or run off by means of a waste pipe, and the plate flooded with water.

The fixing, which does not require the continued presence of the operator, may be accomplished in the changing bag or dark room.

Price for	...	7 × 5	...	...	21/-
,,	..	9 × 7	...	...	27/6

TRADE DISCOUNT LIST ON APPLICATION.

PERKEN, SON, & RAYMENT, 99, Hatton Garden, LONDON.

"OPTIMUS" LAMPS FOR DARK ROOM.

The Lantern shown in the diagram is fitted with a gas jet adjustable from the outside: the light can thereby be readily lessened or increased at will. In front is a sheet of ruby or orange glass, easily removed, behind which is a double thickness of canary fabric set in a metal frame; it is, therefore, safe when developing the most sensitive of plates. As development progresses, one of the non-acting media can be moved, and the negative examined by the protection the second medium continues to give, enabling the amount of detail to be judged with certainty. In this lamp the joints are all perfectly light-tight, being made with a double turn over of tin; the upper parts are also held together with rivets. Ventilation is well considered, as a shaft at the back of the lamp, open at bottom and top, encourages a free circulation of air. Without doubt this lamp has no equal for the purpose for which it is intended.—*British Journal of Photography.*

Fitted either with Gas or Argand Burner for Paraffin Oil.

Square or Round . . .. each 13s.

The form of Lantern shown in the accompanying diagram presents a great many advantages. It possesses a powerful Lamp so arranged that the oil receptacle is isolated from the flame and cannot get heated. Plenty of air circulates. In front is a sheet of ruby glass (removable), behind which is a sheet of deep orange; it is therefore safe when developing the most sensitive of Plates. As development progresses the ruby glass can be raised and the Negative examined by the orange glass only, enabling the amount of detail to be readily judged, per doz. 88/-

FOLDING LAMP.—An inexpensive form of Lamp having two sides of metal, and the third of red glass. The metal sides are hinged together, so that they fold up for travelling, with the ruby glass protected from fracture by lying between them. Top and bottom triangular pieces—one forming a candle-holder and the other a chimney—complete this clever little arrangement ... ... per doz. 30/-

REDDINGS' PATENT PORTABLE LAMP—
Small, 40/-: Medium, 54/-; and Large, 72/-per doz.

CANDLES for above ... ... Small, 28/-; Large ditto, 42/- gross.

TRADE DISCOUNT LIST ON APPLICATION.

PERKEN, SON, & RAYMENT, 99, Hatton Garden, LONDON.

"OPTIMUS" REVOLVING PRINT-WASHER.

Water is injected from a perforated tube which crosses the tank at the bottom. The force of water creates a revolving current which carries the prints over and over in its course. The bottom is slightly V shaped and contains an outlet for waste.

Prices, including Grooved Metal Rack, which fits into the tank and accommodates negatives which can be also washed. Making the machine efficient for both NEGATIVES and PRINTS.

For Negatives and Smaller ... $\frac{1}{4}$, 16/-; $\frac{10}{8}$, 21/-; $\frac{12}{10}$, 30/-

"OPTIMUS" ROCKING PRINT-WASHER.

Water running from a tap revolves the wheel which is connected with the cradle causing it to rock up and down at each revolution. A syphon is fitted to drain the tank. One hour's washing is ample.

inches 9 × 7 cradle **18/6** | 11 × 9 cradle **28/-** | 13 × 11 cradle **32/-**
16 × 13 ,, **39/6** | 20 × 16 ,, **50/-**

NEGATIVE WASHER
AND DRAINING RACK, COMBINED,
For Quarter, Five by Four, Half, and Whole Plate Negatives, **7/9**.

Trade Discount List on Application.

PERKEN, SON, & RAYMENT, 99, Hatton Garden, LONDON

"OPTIMUS"
BURNISHERS FOR PHOTOGRAPHIC PRINTS

The Burnishing Bar is specially hardened. The Frame is of superior and convenient construction. It is Nickel-plated, and of beautiful finish. Each instrument is mounted on a table with legs.

Plate $\tfrac{1}{4}$ $\tfrac{1}{2}$ 1 $1\tfrac{0}{4}$ $1\tfrac{2}{0}$ $1\tfrac{3}{2}$ (larger
Price 20/-   30/-   36/-   45/-   60/-   90/-   to order.)

"OPTIMUS" CAMEO PRESSES.

Carte de Visite (3 shapes) **10/-**
Cabinet (8 shapes each for Cabinet and Carte de Visite)... .. .. **22/.**

TRADE DISCOUNT LIST ON APPLICATION.

PHOTOGRAPHIC SUNDRIES.

Vulcanite Trays.

	3 by 3½	4¾ by 3¾	5¾ by 4½	7 by 5½	8 by 6	9 by 7	11¼ by 9¼ by 1	13½ by 11¼ by 1½
Price per doz.	**5/3**	**5/9**	**6/9**	**8/9**	**15/-**	**19/-**	**27/-**	**46/-**

Porcelain Trays.

	5 by 4	6 by 5	7 by 5	8 by 6	9 by 7	10 by 8	11 by 9	12 by 10	13 by 11	14 by 11
Price per doz.	**7/3**	**8/6**	**9/3**	**10/6**	**12/6**	**15/-**	**20/-**	**25/-**	**35/-**	**42/-**

Papier Mache.

	4¾ by 3	7 by 5	8¾ by 6¾	10¾ by 8¾	12¾ by 10¾	15¼ by 12¾
Price per doz.	**6/9**	**11/-**	**14/-**	**21/-**	**28/6**	**45/-**

Folding Plate Racks.

For draining plates after washing: (to hold 12)	**10/3**	**13/6**	**18/-**
" " (" 24)	**14/-**	**18/-**	**24/-**

Graduated Glass Measures.

	1dr.	2dr.	1oz.	2oz.	4oz	6oz.	8oz.	10oz.	16oz.	20oz.	32oz.	40oz
Per doz.	**6/-**	**7/6**	**6/9**	**8/-**	**10/3**	**12/9**	**14/3**	**15/9**	**22/3**	**27/-**	**40/6**	**45/-**

Glass Funnels, Ribbed or Plain.

Diam of Top Ins.	1½	2	2	3	4	4½	5	5½	6	7	8
Price per doz.	**3/-**	**3/3**	**3/6**	**4/0**	**4/6**	**5/-**	**7/-**	**9/-**	**12/-**	**16/-**	**21/-**

Cutting Shapes.

	C.D.V.	4 by 3	Cabinet.	6½ by 4¾	8½ by 6½	10 by 8	12 by 10
Price per doz.	**5/6**	**6/-**	**9/6**	**10/6**	**22/-**	**36/-**	**48/-**

Trade Discount List on Application.

PERKEN, SON, & RAYMENT, 99, Hatton Garden, LONDON

PHOTOGRAPHIC SUNDRIES.

Printing Frames Oak.

Superior finish, round corners, brass springs, per doz.

4¼ by 3¼	5 by 4	6½ by 4¾	8¼ by 6½	10 by 8	12 by 10
4/9	6/2	8/9	12/6	18/-	27/-

Mahogany, superior, per doz.

9/-	15/-	21/-	32/-	50/-	66/-

Light-tight Plate Boxes.

Mahogany, for 12 plates, per doz.

30/-	43/-	54/0	68/-	78/-	84/-

„ „ 24 „ „

60/-	72/-	80/-	102/6	144/-	180/-

Negative Boxes.

White Wood (to hold 12), per doz.

10/6	12/-	18/-	22/6	37/6	45/-

„ „ 24), „

12/9	13/6	22/6	28/-	40/-	57/-

„ „ 50), „

16/6	21/-	28/6	39/-	57/-	66/-

Vignette Glasses.

6/6	12/6	18/-	25/6	30/-	48/-

Carriers or Inner Frames.

For Double Dark Slides, to carry smaller plates, per doz.

15/9	18/-	21/-	27/-	36/-	48/

TRADE DISCOUNT LIST ON APPLICATION.

PERKEN, SON, & RAYMENT, 99, Hatton Garden, LONDON.

"OPTIMUS" ENLARGING APPARATUS.

This Apparatus comprises superior Mahogany Body Lantern and long Bellows Camera adjusted by Patent Quick Action Rack and Pinion. The Lantern is fitted with powerful Refulgent Lamp, with 3 wicks, giving brilliant illumination. Compound Condensers.

CONDENSER.

5-inch no front lens	...	100/-
5 ,, with ,,	...	127/-
6 ,, no ,,	...	133/-
6 ,, with ,,	...	151/-
7 ,, no ,,	...	155/-
7 ,, with ,,	...	173/6
8 ,, with ,,	...	256/-
9 ,, with ,,	...	290/-
10 ,, with ,,	...	360/-
12 ,, with ,,	...	580/-

If with Russian Iron instead of Mahogany Body.

5inch no lens	...	75/-
5 ,, and ,,	...	102/6
6 ,, no ,,	...	87/6
6 ,, and ,,	...	115/3
7 ,, no ,,	...	110/-
7 ,, and ,,	...	137/9
8 ,, no ,,	...	160/-
9		210/-
10 ,, ,, ,,	...	285/-
12 ,, ,, ,,	..	450/-

Adapted for use with Lime-light or Oil Lamp.

When large sized Condensers are employed, it will be found advantageous to use the Oxy-hydrogen or Oxy-calcium Lime Light Burners; but good results are obtained with the Refulgent Mineral Oil Lamps supplied with the apparatus.

'OPTIMUS' COMPOUND CONDENSERS (mounted) FOR ENLARGEMENTS.

Inches Diameter	3½	4	4½	5	6	7	8	9	10	12
	8/-	8/6	16/6	24/-	39/-	50/9	69/6	93/6	132/-	222/-

TRADE DISCOUNT LIST ON APPLICATION.

PERKEN, SON, & RAYMENT, 99, Hatton Garden, LONDON.

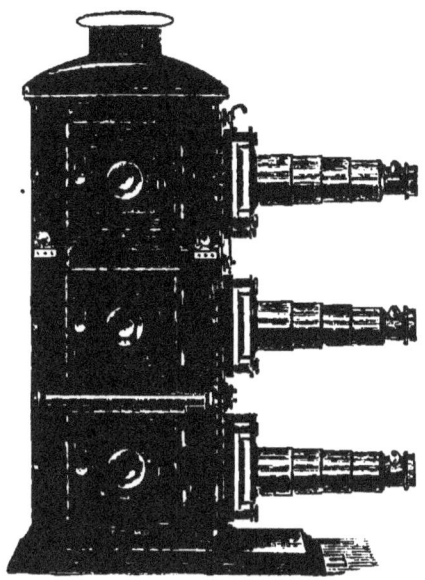

'OPTIMUS'
TRIPLE OXY-HYDROGEN LANTERN

The Top of the Lantern may be used separately with Oil Lamp.

Seasoned Mahogany Body, 6 Panelled Doors with Sight Holes. Moulded foot, picked out with black, Highly Finished Brass Stages and Sliding Tubes, Compound Condensers 4 inches diameter. Three-draw Telescopic Front Tubes, and SIX Photographic Front Lenses of 6-in. and 4-in. focus ... 22 18 0
Three Safety Gas Jets 1 13 0
'OPTIMUS' Triple Dissolving Tap (Patent) 1 13 0

£26 4 0

The Draw Tubes are specially rigid, so maintaining the Optical Axis accurately and ensuring the Front Lens, Condenser, and Slide occupying Parallel Planes.
**Curtain Slide, extra 7/-; Double pinion, extra 3/-; Flashers, extra 3/6 each.
Lantern Photographs,** ... ... Plain, 12/-; Coloured, 18/6 per doz.

TRADE DISCOUNT LIST ON APPLICATION.

PERKEN, SON, & RAYMENT, 99, Hatton Garden, LONDON.

'OPTIMUS'
OXY-HYDROGEN TRIPLE LANTERN.

The Top Lantern may be used separately with Oil Lamp ·

Seasoned Mahogany body, 6 Panelled Doors with Sight holes. Moulded foot, picked out with black, Finished Brass Stages and Sliding Tubes. Achromatic Photographic Combination Front Lenses, large diameter Back Lens, Compound Condensers of 4 inches diameter 14 10 0
3 Safety Gas Jets 1 13 0
'OPTIMUS' Triple Dissolving Tap (Patent) 1 13 0

Complete   £17 16 0

The Draw Tubes are made specially rigid, so maintaining the optical axis accurately and ensuring the front lens, condenser and slide occupying parallel planes.

**Curtain Slide, extra 7/-; Double pinion, extra 3/-; Flashers, extra 3/6 each.
Lantern Photographs,** ... ... Plain, 12/-; Coloured, 18/6 per doz.

TRADE DISCOUNT LIST ON APPLICATION.

PERKEN, SON, & RAYMENT, 99, Hatton Garden, LONDON.

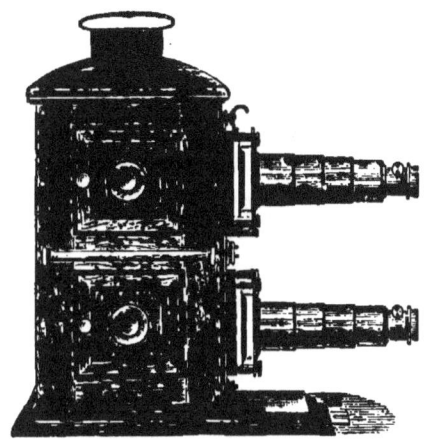

'OPTIMUS' BI-UNIAL OXY-HYDROGEN LANTERN.

Seasoned Mahogany Body, 4 Panelled Doors with Sight Ho'es, Moulded Foot, picked out with Black, Compound Bi-convex Condensers of 4 inches diameter. Highly Finished Brass Stages, and with Brass 3-draw Telescopic Front Tubes, and FOUR Photographic Front Lenses of 6 inches, 4 inches focus ... ... £14 14s.

2 Safety Jets ... ... £1 2s.
6 Way Dissolving Tap ... ... 17s.

£16 13s.

The Draw Tubes are specially rigid, so maintaining the Optical Axis accurately, and ensuring the Front Lens, Condenser, and Slide occupying Parallel Planes.

Curtain Slide, extra 7/-; Double pinion, extra 3/-; Flashers, extra 3/6 each.
Lantern Photographs, ... Plain, 12'-; Coloured, 18/6 per doz.

TRADE DISCOUNT LIST ON APPLICATION.

PERKEN, SON, & RAYMENT, 99, Hatton Garden, LONDON.

'OPTIMUS' BI-UNIAL LANTERN

For Oxy-Hydrogen Lime Light.

The Top Lantern may be used with Oil Lamp.

Seasoned Mahogany Body, 4 Panelled Doors with Sight Holes, moulded foot picked out with black, Japanned stages and tubes, Achromatic Photographic Front Lenses, compound condensers of 4 inches diameter **£5 12 0**

Ditto ditto with highly finished BRASS stages and sliding tubes... **8 8 0**

The Draw Tubes are specially rigid, so maintaining the Optical Axis accurately and ensuring the Front Lens, Condenser, and Slide occupying Parallel Planes.

**Curtain Slide, extra 7/-; Double pinion, extra 3/-; Flashers, extra 3/6 each.
Lantern Photographs,** ... ... Plain, 12/-; Coloured, 18/6 per doz.

TRADE DISCOUNT LIST ON APPLICATION.

PERKEN, SON, & RAYMENT, 99, Hatton Garden, LONDON.

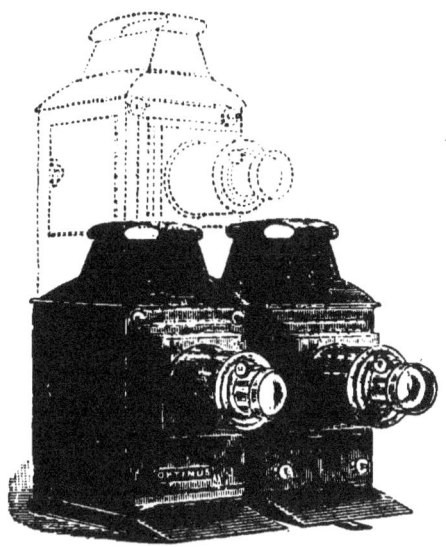

'OPTIMUS' SIDE-BY-SIDE OR BI-UNIAL MAGIC LANTERN.

May be used as a pair with Oil or Lime-light.

The above Diagram represents a full-sized combined Lantern. It is made of japanned metal. It may be worked one above the other, as the dotted lines show, or side by side as the positive diagram shows : or again, the two Instruments may be separated and worked in two distinct places, as each Lantern is complete in itself. A further advantage is possessed by these Lanterns, for the body which is constructed to accommodate limelight will also readily accommodate oil lamps, the groove into which the trays are inserted being made to the same guage as our Lamps.

Without Lamps or Jets £4 19 0
Gas Jets ... ... each... 11 0
3-Wick Lamps, each 12 0
Achromatic Photographic Combination Front Lenses (with large diameter Back Lens). Compound Condensers of 4 inches diameter.
Curtain Slide, extra 7/-; Double pinion, extra 3/-; Flashers, extra 3/6 each.
Lantern Photographs, ... Plain, 12/-; Coloured, 18/6 per doz.

TRADE DISCOUNT LIST ON APPLICATION.

PERKEN, SON, & RAYMENT, 99, Hatton Garden, LONDON

'OPTIMUS' MAGIC LANTERN.
Japanned Metal Body **30/-**
Adapted for use with Limelight. For Dissolving 2 Lanterns are necessary.

STUDENT'S MAGIC LANTERN.
Students Lantern Japanned Metal Body (to take demonstrating tank)
with finished Brass Sliding Tubes **40/-**
Do. Russian Iron Body, with finished brass front stage
plate and sliding tube **55/-**
Adapted for use with Limelight. For Dissolving, 2 Lanterns are necessary.
Each Magic Lantern is efficient for exhibitions. The Lens gives crisp definition, being a superior Achromatic Photographic Combination (large diameter back lens). with rack and pinion. It is fitted to a telescopic lengthening tube, so gaining increased focal accommodation. The Condenser is composed of two plano-convex lenses of 4 inches diameter The refulgent lamp has 8 wicks, or 4 wicks 2s. extra, yielding a brilliantly illuminated picture.—Each is complete in box.

TRADE DISCOUNT LIST ON APPLICATION.

PERKEN, SON, & RAYMENT, 99, Hatton Garden, LONDON

RUSSIAN IRON MAGIC LANTERN.
Highly Finished Brass Sliding Tubes ... . **45s.**
Adapted for use with Limelight. For Dissolving, 2 Lanterns are necessary.

Each Magic Lantern is efficient for exhibitions. The Lens gives crisp definition, being a superior Achromatic Photographic Combination (large diameter back lens), with rack and pinion. It is fitted to a telescopic lengthening tube, so gaining increased focal accommodation. The Condenser is composed of two plano-convex lenses of 4 inches diameter. The refulgent lamp has 3 wicks, or 4 wicks 2s. extra, yielding a brilliantly illuminated picture.—Each is complete in box.

"OPTIMUS" MAGIC LANTERNS.
Perforated Russian Iron Body, Brass Sliding Tubes ... **50s.**
Adapted for use with Limelight. For Dissolving 2 Lanterns are necessary.

Each Magic Lantern is efficient for exhibitions. The Lens gives crisp definition, being a superior Achromatic Photographic Combination (large diameter back lens), with rack and pinion. It is fitted to a telescopic lengthening tube, so gaining increased focal accommodation. The Condenser is composed of two plano-convex lenses of 4 inches diameter. The refulgent lamp has 3 wicks, or 4 wicks 2s. extra, yielding a brilliantly illuminated picture.—Each is complete in box.

TRADE DISCOUNT LIST ON APPLICATION.

PERKEN, SON, & RAYMENT, 99, Hatton Garden, LONDON.

"OPTIMUS" MAHOGANY MAGIC LANTERN.
Mahogany outside Body, Japanned Metal Stages and Sliding Tubes ... **42s.**

**"OPTIMUS"
SUPERIOR MAHOGANY MAGIC LANTERN.**
Seasoned Mahogany Body, 2 Panelled Doors, Highly Finished Brass Stages and Sliding Tubes ... ... **82s.**
Adapted for use with Limelight. For Dissolving, 2 Lanterns are necessary.

Each Magic Lantern is efficient for exhibitions. The Lens gives crisp definition, being a superior Achromatic Photographic Combination (large diameter back lens), with rack and pinion. It is fitted to a telescopic lengthening tube, so gaining increased focal accommodation. The Condenser is composed of two plano convex lenses of 4 inches diameter. The refulgent lamp has 3 wicks, or 4 wicks 2s. extra, yielding a brilliantly illuminated picture.—Each is complete in box.

TRADE DISCOUNT LIST ON APPLICATION.

PERKEN, SON, & RAYMENT, 99, Hatton Garden, LONDON.

'OPTIMUS'
PAIRS OF LANTERNS FOR DISSOLVING.

For Dissolving Views, two Lanterns are required, and are arranged in one portable box; either of the before mentioned styles of Lanterns may be selected. The extra cost above that of the two lanterns being 8/0, the price of the fan dissolver; if used for oxy-hydrogen light two gas jets are needed.

Japanned Metal Body ...	30/-	each.
,, ,, Student's Form	40/-	,,
Mahogany Body, Lined with Metal	42/-	,,
Russian Iron Body	45/-	,,
,, ,, Perforated	50/-	,,
,, ,, Student	55/-	,,
Seasoned Mahogany Body, 2 Panelled Doors, all Brass Fittings	82/-	,,

Each Magic Lantern is efficient for exhibitions. The Lens gives crisp definition, being a superior Achromatic Photographic Combination (large diameter back lens), with rack and pinion. It is fitted to a telescopic lengthening tube, so gaining increased focal accommodation. The Condenser is composed of two plano-convex lenses 4 inches diameter. The refulgent lamp has 3 wicks (or 4 wicks, 2s. extra), yielding a brilliantly illuminated picture.— Each is complete in box.

Safety Blow through Gas Jets	11/-	each.
Chamber (mixed) ,, ,,	16/6	,,
Lantern Photographs, Plain, 12/-; Coloured, 18/6 per doz.		

TRADE DISCOUNT LIST ON APPLICATION.

PERKEN, SON, & RAYMENT, 99, Hatton Garden, LONDON.

'OPTIMUS' MAGIC LANTERNS FOR YOUTHS.
To burn Paraffin or Mineral Oil.

The body of these lanterns is so constructed that the oil reservoir is not like'y to become heated, since it falls through the bottom of the illuminated chamber and is in outside air.

Small Magic Lanterns, with condensers, front lens (adjustable), black japanned body, chimney, lamp and reflector—

No. 1	... diam. front lens	$1\frac{1}{8}$	... condenser	$1\frac{3}{4}$	...	2,6 each
2	... ,,	$1\frac{1}{4}$	... ,,	$1\frac{3}{4}$	...	3 10 ,,
3	... ,,	$1\frac{5}{16}$	... ,,	$2\frac{1}{16}$	...	6/6 ,,
4	... ,,	$1\frac{1}{2}$	... ,,	$2\frac{1}{8}$	...	9/- ,,
5	... ,,	$1\frac{1}{2}$	... ,,	3	...	11/- ,,
6 (in box)	,,	$1\frac{5}{8}$	... ,,	$3\frac{1}{2}$	...	20/- ,,

Boxes of 12 Slides for Lantern, each Slide containing several figures arranged as Tales if desired.

No. 1	Paper edge	...	3/- each.
2	,,	...	3/8
3	Wood edge	...	6/8
4	,,	...	9 4
5	,,	...	12/-
6	,,	...	16/-
7	,,	...	18/8

NOTE.—We maintain the sizes, both of Lanterns and Slides, as of old: many makers call our No. 2 No. 3, and so on.

TRADE DISCOUNT LIST ON APPLICATION.

PERKEN, SON, & RAYMENT, 99, Hatten Garden, LONDON.

RACKWORK & MECHANICAL SLIDES.
For Lanterns with 4 inch Compound Condensers only.

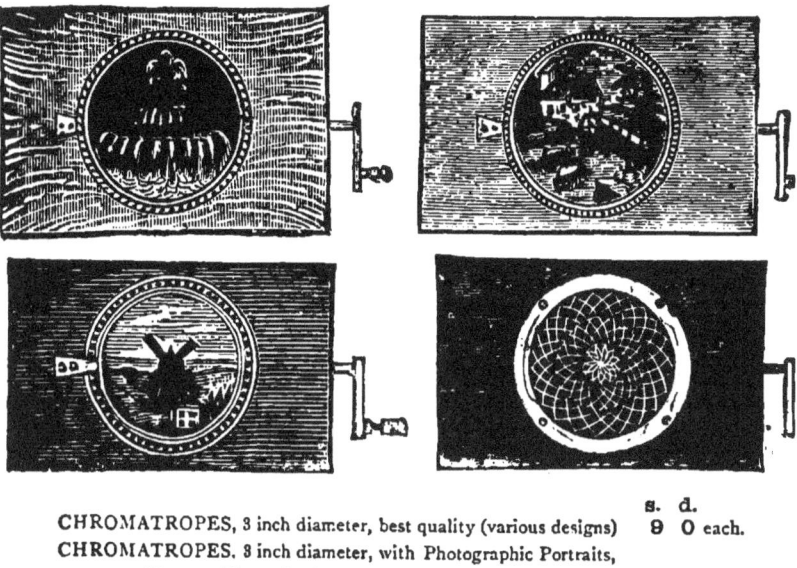

	s.	d.
CHROMATROPES, 3 inch diameter, best quality (various designs)	9	0 each.
CHROMATROPES. 3 inch diameter, with Photographic Portraits, Mottoes, Views, &c. in centre	10	0 ,,
CHROMATROPE CARRIER FRAME, with 6 Pairs of Painted Discs in rack box	21	0 ,,
RACKWORK SOLDIERS' HEADS, changing to Donkeys' Heads	8	6 ,,
SNOWSTORM EFFECT	7	0 ,,
CURTAIN to roll up, showing Painted Curtain or Drop Scene	10	0 ,,
DANCING SKELETON SLIDE, with lever motion taking off Head	5	0 ,,
LIGHTNING EFFECT	1	9 ,,
RAINBOW EFFECT	1	9 ,,
LEVER MOON-RISING EFFECT	4	6 ,,
MAN SWALLOWING RATS, rack mills, &c.	10	0 ,,
RACK WORK, best painted wave slides	15	0 ,,

TRADE DISCOUNT LIST ON APPLICATION.

PERKEN, SON, & RAYMENT, 99, Hatten Garden, LONDON.

SLIDING CARRIER BLOCK.

	s.	d.
For two pictures, per doz.	27	0
SETS OF EFFECT SLIDES for dissolving views from... per set	4	6
Sets of all the most popular Nursery Tales, in great variety best painted ... ... per slide...	4	0
Second quality ... ... per slide...	2	8
LONG PANORAMA SLIDES .... from...each...	2	3
Motto Slides ... ... ,, ,, ...	3	0
SETS OF 10 SLIDES, best rack Astronomy, 2¼-inch circles, in mahogany box	100	0
Ditto ditto in 3-inch ,, ,,	110	0
PHOTOGRAPHIC VIEWS taken in all countries per dozen	12	0
Colored ditto ... ... from per dozen	18	6
SQUARE WOOD BLOCKS, per gross	42	0
Soft limes, per tin of one dozen	1	0
Hard limes	1	6
Front lenses for lantern, rack motion, double achromatic photographic combination...	15	0
Ditto ditto long focus	36	0
,, ,, ,, ,, ...	46	0
GAS JETS.		
Blow Through	11	0
Chamber	16	6
Interchangeable	18	6

GAS BAGS, GAS CYLINDERS,
At lowest market prices.

SOLE AGENTS FOR THE

PATENT FANTOCCINI ANIMATED TRANSPARENT FIGURES

Which without doubt give a most life-like effect when projected on the screen.

MAGIC LANTERN SLIDES IN GREAT VARIETY.

TRADE DISCOUNT LIST ON APPLICATION.

PERKEN, SON, & RAYMENT, 99, Hatton Garden, LONDON.

COMIC SLIPPING SLIDES.

600 Different Subjects ... ... per doz. **12/-**

These are well painted, giving brilliancy and transparency of colour.

COMIC LEVER SLIDES.

300 Different Subjects ... ... per doz. **37/6**

These mechanical slides are suited for Lanterns with 4-inch condensers.

SLIDING CARRIER BLOCK, for two pictures, per doz. ... **27/-**

TRADE DISCOUNT LIST ON APPLICATION.

PERKEN, SON, & RAYMENT, 99, Hatton Garden, LONDON.

MICROSCOPE FOR LANTERN.

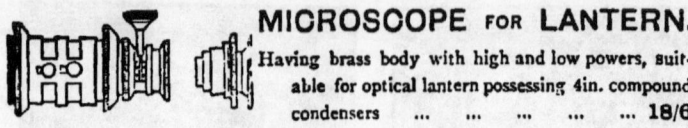

Having brass body with high and low powers, suitable for optical lantern possessing 4in. compound condensers **18/6**

MICROSCOPE FOR L'ANTERN.

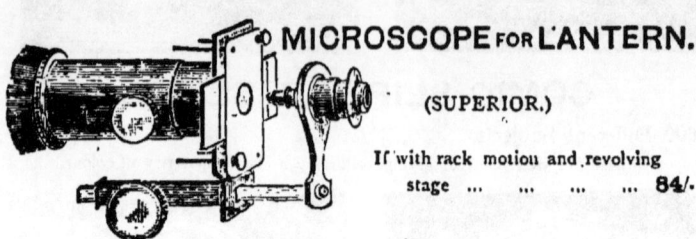

(SUPERIOR.)

If with rack motion and revolving stage **84/-**

"OPTIMUS" APHENGESCOPE.

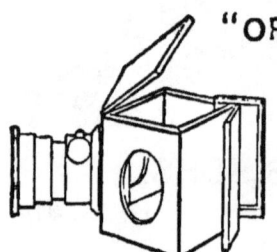

An instrument for exhibiting opaque objects, cartes-de-visite, etc.; suitable for optical lantern with 4in. compound condensers **16/-**

Superior Aphengescope, arranged for pairs of lanterns with achromatic front lenses and rack adjustments **30/-**

"OPTIMUS" POLARISCOPE

With analyser in case **105/-**

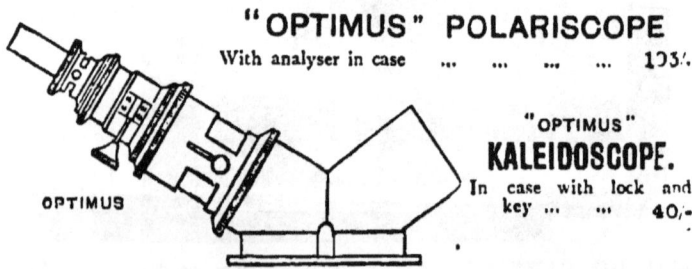

"OPTIMUS"
KALEIDOSCOPE.
In case with lock and key **40/-**

OPTIMUS

TRADE DISCOUNT LIST ON APPLICATION.

PERKEN, SON, & RAYMENT, 99, Hatton Garden, LONDON.

"OPTIMUS" REFULGENT LAMPS.
Stout Russian Iron.   Burning Mineral Oil.

This lamp has been universally pronounced the *safest* yet the *most brilliant* lamp used with the Projecting Magic Lantern. A flame-sight-hole at the back enables the manipulator to adjust the wicks with the nicest accuracy whilst working.

Two wicks (wicks 2 inches wide)	12/6
Three wicks	13/6
Four wicks	15/6

"OPTIMUS" LAMP WICK TRIMMER (Patent).

For 1½ inch wicks	2/6
For 2 inch wicks	4/9

This little contrivance saves much trouble. With one cut it cleans off the charred portion of wick, and leaves a perfectly even ridge of cotton to hold the flame, which, in consequence, burns with a clearness and freedom from smoke that is very desirable. It is particularly recommended for photographic developing lamps, and for lamps used with the optical lantern.—*British Journal of Photography.*

ANIMALCULÆ OR CHEMICAL TANK.
These being made of Glass and Indiarubber, are not affected by chemicals   3/6

DISCOUNTS ON APPLICATION.

PERKEN, SON, & RAYMENT, 99, Hatton Garden, LONDON.

MAGIC LANTERN GAS JETS FOR LIMELIGHT.

Best quality blow-through gas jet, with cog-wheel arrangement for turning, also raising and lowering the lime; platina nipple ... ... each 11/-

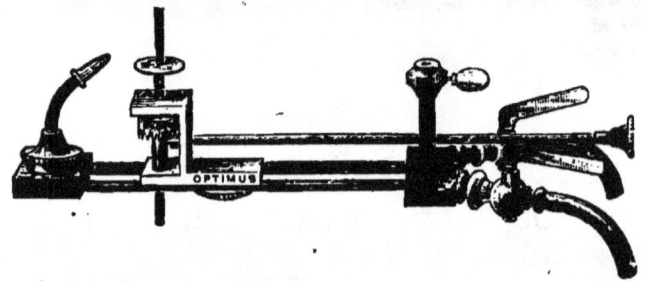

Best mixed chamber gas jet, with cog-wheel arrangement for turning, also raising and lowering the lime; platina nipple ... ... each 16/6

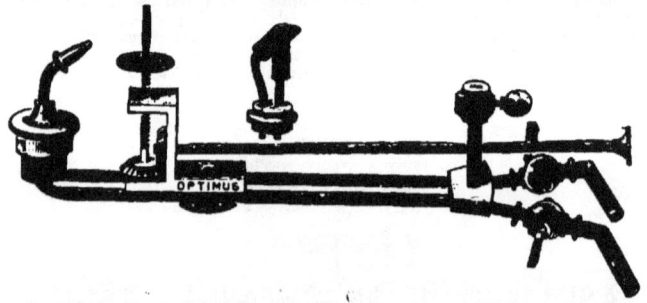

New interchangeable jet or both gases under pressure, mixed or for blow-through form, by simply removing and using the burner as required; both have platina nipples ... ... each 18/9

TRADE DISCOUNT LIST ON APPLICATION.

PERKEN, SON, & RAYMENT, 99, Hatton Garden, LONDON.

ZINC
PURIFIER,
4/-

BRAZED
IRON
RETORT,
10/-

GAS CYLINDER
With Regulator and Pressure Gauge attached.

GAS BAGS—Stout Twill.

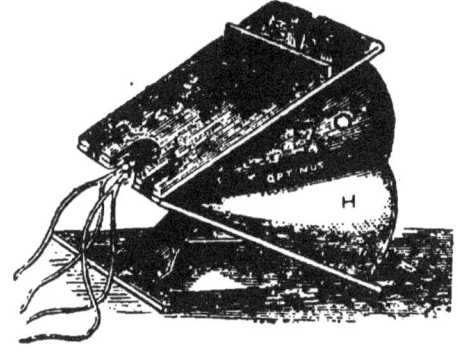

	SIZES.		Capacity	
in.	in.	in.	cubic ft.	Price
30 by 24 by 20			4	32/-
26	24	20	5	37/6
30	24	24	6	39/6
36	28	24	7	42/-
30	32	24	8	45/-
36	36	24	9	46/6
40	32	24	9	48/6
40	36	24	10	51/-
40	36	20	11	53/-
40	36	28	12	55/-

Subject to Fluctuations.

TRADE DISCOUNT LIST ON APPLICATION.

PERKEN, SON, & RAYMENT, 99, Hatton Garden, LONDON.

PATENT SAFETY POROUS
ETHER SATURATOR,
FOR PRODUCING THE
ETHO-OXYGEN LIME LIGHT,
FOR OPTICAL LANTERNS.

This Apparatus is the **most perfect** means for producing the Etho-Oxygen Lime Light, and gives the most powerful illumination known for Optical Lanterns. In its use there is no heat, no bubbling, and no obstruction to the free passage of the Oxygen. It can be disturbed or upset without affecting the light or spilling any Ether into the tubing. After one adjustment of the light, it will automatically regulate the supply of Ether vapour to correspond to any variation in the supply of Oxygen. **This is a very important advantage possessed by no other Apparatus.**

ILLUSTRATION.

a To Ether side of Jet.   *b* To Oxygen side of Jet.   T Piece—to Bag.

It consists of two brass tubes or bodies, screwed into a bent brass connecting tube, lying side by side on an ebonised wooden stand, which is fitted with a handle for carrying about. The brass tubes or bodies can easily be removed by unscrewing the set screws which fasten them to the board. Each tube is fitted at one end with screw-down cap, having a nozzle in its centre for the purpose of attaching elastic tubing, and both are fitted with a roll of flannel or coarse cloth, having a spiral wire in the centre to keep them open. Each nozzle has a small screw cap to prevent escape of Ether when not in use.

PRICE 36,-

TRADE DISCOUNT LIST ON APPLICATION.

PERKEN, SON, & RAYMENT, 99, Hatton Garden, LONDON.

TRANSPARENT SCREENS. Best Union Cloth.

Feet square	6	7	10	12	14	16	20
	27/-	28/-	30/-	36/-	45/-	60/-	75/- 126/-

"OPTIMUS" (LECTURER'S) PORTABLE READING LAMP.

Price of Lamp, with Signal, Bell, and Match Box complete ... ... 8/- each

TRADE DISCOUNT LIST ON APPLICATION.

PERKEN, SON, & RAYMENT, 99, Hatton Garden, LONDON.

SETS OF LANTERN
PHOTOGRAPHS.

Price Uncoloured .. .. 12s. per dozen.
" Coloured .. .. 18s. 6d. "
Number of Slides comprised in each Set is stated in figures attached to each Title.

A

A Day in London .. ... set of	60
A Day's Holiday at Windsor ...	30
A Photographer's Perplexities ...	12
A Precious Couple on the road to Gretna Green	12
A Trap to Catch a Sunbeam ...	15
A Trip to Brighton...	40
A true Story of the old Coaching Days	10
A Visit to the British Museum ...	50
A Walk in the "Zoo"	48
A Year within the Arctic Circle...	50
Abbeys and Castles of England ..	50
Adventures of Briggs with a Bull	4
Adventures of Brown, Smith, Jones and Robinson	4
Æsop's Fables	50
Afghan War...	36
Aladdin, or the Wonderful Lamp	107
Algiers	20
Alice in Wonderland	42
" " Songs ...	7
America, North, and Niagara ...	59
American Franklin Search Expedition	20
Androcles and the Lion	6
Animal Sagacity	24
Animals at the Zoological Gardens	215
An Old Story	26
Art Collections, South Kensington Museum	50
Astronomy ... ... }	300
Astronomical Instruments · }	

B

Baby's Sugar Bag	12
Barber and his Clever Dog ...	12
Baron Munchausen	8
" "	17
Barred Window	8
Bashful Man...	6
Beautiful Snow ... ... ,..	5
Belgium ... .; ...	50
Berlin...	46
Bible Manners and Custom ...	30
Blunderbore.. ·	12
Book of Martyrs ... ·. ..	52
Bookworm...	12

B (continued).

Boons and Blessings	16
Bottle, The	8
Boys and Ravens	8
Boys of Corinth	12
Brazilian Ape	14
Brighton Aquarium	·14
Briggs and the Bull	78
British Museum, Antiquities of &c.	28
Brown and the Bear	12
Brown and Mouse	12
Brussels	50
Bunyan, Life of	111
Bunyan's Pilgrim's Progress "Art Journal"	22
Do. Cassell	36
Bunyan's Pilgrim's Progress Religious Tract Society, set of	17
Do. Routledge	111
Do. Service of Song	38
Do. Christiana	32
Burglars, The Two..	12
Burnah	36
Buy your Own Goose	6
Buy your Own Cherries ... ...7 & 10

C

Canada from Quebec to the Rocky Mountains	60
Cats and Serpents	8
Cathedrals, Our English	50
Cat, Nine Lives of a	12
Central Africa	50
Children in the Wood	8
Channel Islands	60
Children's Entertainment, 1 ...	48
" " 2 ...	48
Children's Messiah, Service of Song	32
Chimes, The ... .·	24
China and the Chinese ..· ...	60
Christmas Set	17
Christie's Old Organ ... 24 & 17
Cinderella	8
Cleopatra's Needle...	47
Clever Nephew	12
Cock Robin	8
Come Home, Father	3

Price of above Lantern Photographs: Plain 12/-, Coloured 18/6 per doz.

TRADE DISCOUNT LIST ON APPLICATION,

PERKEN, SON, & RAYMENT, 99, Hatton Garden, LONDON

SETS OF LANTERN PHOTOGRAPHS.

C (continued).

Comic Slipping Slides	100
Cornwall	50
Crochet's Musical Recital... ...	12
Cruikshank's Works	28
Crusoe, Robinson	17
"Curfew must not ring to-night"	10
Colony of New Zealand. Part 1	54
„ „ „ 2	39

D

Lume Perkins and her Grey Mare	8
Dan Dabberton's Dream	14
Day in London	60
Dear Father, Come Home ...	8
Death of the Bluebottle	12
Devonshire	50
Dickens' Chimes	24
Dick Whittington ... .21 &	8
Diogenes and the Boys of Corinth	12
Donkey and Mill	12
Doré's Bible Illustrations... ...	250
Dr. Spiritus and the Moon ...	8
Dreams at Sea	5
Drunkard's Children	8
„ Progress	14
Ducks and Frog	12

E

Egypt .. .. set of	60
Egypt, Modern, and its People ...	50
Egyptian War, The	50
Elephant's Revenge	12
Engadine Switzerland, The ...	50
English Cathedrals...	50
English Lakes	50
English River Scenery	50
Eva	26

F

Fables, Æsop's	50
„ La Fontaine's	135
Five Senses	5
Flea, Adventures with a	12
Fly, Adventures with a	12
Florence, The City of	36
Foolish Toper	12
Four Seasons	4
Foxe's Book of Martyrs	52
Friendless Bob	18

G

Gabriel Grub	17
General Description and Statistics of London	48
General Gordon	24
Gilpin, Johnny	12
Gin Fiend	4
Gin Shop	12
Golden Goose	12
Gossips	12
Greatest Plague of Life	12
Groups and Ideal Photos. from Life	80

H

Haddon Hall	18
Hardanger Fjord Norway, The...	41
Heat	200
Heathen Chinee	9
Highlands of Scotland, The ..	52
Holland	50
History of a Pound of Tea ...	10
„ a Cotton Bale	10
„ a Quartern Loaf ...	10
„ a Pound of Sugar ...	10
„ a Golden Sovereign ..	10
„ a Scuttle of Coals ...	10
Hogarth's Works	50
„ Harlot's Progress, The	6
„ Industry and Idleness	12
„ Marriage à la Mode ...	6
„ Rake's Progress, The	8
„ Reward of Cruelty ...	4
„ Rumours of an Election	4
Holy Land	60
Honey Stealers	8
Hostile Neighbours	12
Housebreakers, The	12
Human Physiology	52
Hunting Expedition, H.R.H. the Prince of Wales ... 30 &	30
Hymns,Christie's Old Organ,set of	17
Hymns, Words only	300

I

Impulsive Gardener	8
India, Mysore	51
Introductory Slides to various subjects	46
Introductory Slides and Mottoes	43
Inverted World	6
Ireland, 1	60
„ 2	50
Italy	50
Italian Lakes	50

Price of above Lantern Photographs: Plain 12/-, Coloured 18/6 per doz.

TRADE DISCOUNT LIST ON APPLICATION.

PERKEN, SON, & RAYMENT, 99, Hatton Garden, LONDON.

SETS OF LANTERN PHOTOGRAPHS.

J, K

Jack and the Beanstalk	8
Jack the Conqueror	12
Jack the Giant Killer	8
Jackdaw of Rheims	13
Jane Conquest	16
Jessica's First Prayer	10 & 18
Jocko the Brazilian Ape	14
John Hampden's Home	6
Johnny Gilpin	12
John Ploughman's Pictures	38
John Ploughman's Picture Hymns	17
John Tregenoweth: his Mark	18
Jones' Baby	4
Joseph, Service of Song	33
Juvenile Smokers	6
Kate Maloney	6

L

La Fontaine's Fables	135
Lady Jane Grey	4
Lakes, English	50
" Italian	50
Lazy Traveller	12
Level Crossing	9
Life Boat	7
Life of Martin Luther	12
Light	300
Little Artist and Large Portfolio	8
Little Jim the Collier Boy	6
Little Red Riding Hood	8
Little Tiz	14
Little Town of Weinsburgh	6
Liverpool	42
London Street Traffic	79
London and Neighbourhood	932
London to Rome	50
London to the Falls of Niagara	46
Lovechase and his Dog Tray	12

M

Mad Umbrella	12
Marley's Ghost, a Christmas Carol	25
Mary, Queen of Scots	24
Mary, the Maid of the Inn	10
{ Magnetism and Electricity	33
{ Magnetic Curves	60
Man and Calf	12
Maps ... et of	21
Martin Luther	12
Mechanics, Hydrostatics, &c.	110
Mediterranean	50
Meg and her Brother Ben	13
Messiah, Service of Song	32
Microscopic Gems	50
Microscopical Objects	150
Midnight Adventures with a Flea	12

M (continued).

Miller and the Sweep	12
Mines and Miners	130
Mines and Mining	41
Miss Popp's Pet	12
Mistletoe Bough	7
Modern Egypt	50
Morrow of the Carouse	8
Mother's Last Words	6 & 12
Mottoes and Texts	140
Mouse, Midnight Adventures with	12

N

Nelly's Dark Days	14
New Arctic Expedition	9
New Hat	9
Newton, Sir Isaac, and the Apple	8
New York	50
New York to the White Mountains	60
Niagara	50, 41, 46
Nine Lives of a Cat	12
North American Scenery	143
Norway	40

O

Oiled Feather	12
Old Curiosity Shop, The	24
Old Man and his Ass	7
Old Mother Hubbard	8
Old Story	26
Old Testament Scriptures, Reading	40
Origin of Jones' Baby	4
O'Toole and the Umbrella	9
Outcast London; or, How the Poor Live	40
Our West African Settlements	48
Oxford Colleges	78
Oxford to London Bridge	50

P

Parasites and their Hosts	40
Paris	50
Passions, The	12
Passion Play	50
Peasant and his Ass	7
Peep into Nature through the Microscope, A	54
Phonograph	134
Photographic Sketches of English Life and Scenery	40
Photograph of a Lightning Flash	1
Plant Life	39
Portraits	39

Price of above Lantern Photographs: Plain 12/-, Coloured 18/6 per doz.

TRADE DISCOUNT LIST ON APPLICATION.

PERKEN, SON, & RAYMENT, 99, Hatton Garden, LONDON.

SETS OF LANTERN PHOTOGRAPHS.

P *(continued).*

Power of Music ... ... set of	6
Prince of Wales's Animals at the Zoo	17
Hunting Expedition at Nepaul	30
Prodigal Son, Service of Song ...	38
Professor Crotchet's Musical Recital	12
Progress of Intemperance ...	6
Pussy's Road to Ruin	12

Q

Quarrelsome Dog	12
Quartette Party	9
Queen's Jubilee, 1887	50

R

Retaliation	12
Return from the Tavern, The ...	4
Reward of Covetousness	8
Reward of Cruelty	4
Reynard the Fox	12
Rhine...	60
Rip Van Winkle	12
Rival Lovers	12
Riviera, The	50
Robinson Crusoe	17
Robbers	12
Romance of History	44
Rome	50
Rome, Ancient and Modern ...	50
Round the World with a Camera	60
Round the World in a Yacht ...	45

S

Sambo's Five Senses	5
Sankey's Hymns (Words only) ...	76
Sayings of Jesus, Service of Song	29
Scripture, Old Testament ...	154
" " Joseph	124
Scripture, New Testament ...	77
Scripture Texts	76
Scrub, the Workhouse Boy ...	11
Seasons	4
Serpents and the Cat	8
Service of Song, Eva	26
" " Joseph	33
" " Messiah	32
" " Prodigal Son ...	38
" " Pilgrim's Progress	33
" " Sayings of Jesus	29

S *(continued).*

Seven Ages of Man	7
Signal Box	6
Simon and his Pig	12
Sir Isaac Newton and the Apple	8
Sir John the Giant Slayer ...	24
Sketches, English Life and Scenery	40
Sledge Party	12
Sleepy Hollow	6
Snow-white	7
Scotland	102
Solar System	50
Soldier's Dream, The ... set of	8
Soudan War	57
Sound	177
South Kensington Museum, Art Collections	50
Spain	50
Spectrum Analysis	100
Stanley in Africa	20 & 29
Statuary	78 & 113
Statuary in South Kensington Museum	50
Stolen Sausage	9
Sultan of Ragobaga	15
Suspicious Travellers	12
Switzerland, Tour No. 1	50
" " No. 2	50

T

Tabernacle in the Wilderness ...	15
Tale of a Tub, Set of	7
" " Set of	12
Temperance Mottoes	93
The Chimes	24
The Cottar's Saturday Night ...	9
The Jackdaw of Rheims	13
The Knight and the Lady ...	6
The Old Curiosity Shop	24
The Pied Piper of Hamelin ...	12
The Temperance Sketch Book ...	32
The Three Bears	8
The Vagabonds	10
The Well of St. Keyne	4
The Witch's Frolic	12
The Life Boat	7
The Quaker and the Robber ...	4
The Signal Box	6
The Quartette Party	9
The Baby's Sugar Bag	12
The Rhine	60
The Women of Mumbles Head ...	8
Three Kittens that lost their Mittens	9
Through Turkestan to the Afghan Frontier ... ... set of	50

Price of above Lantern Photographs: Plain 12/-, Coloured 18/6 per doz.

TRADE DISCOUNT LIST ON APPLICATION.

PERKEN, SON, & RAYMENT, 99, Hatton Garden, LONDON.

SETS OF LANTERN PHOTOGRAPHS.

T *(continued).*

Tipsy Geese	6
Toothache	12
Tower of London, The	20
Travels of the Sultan of Ragobaga	15
Trap to Catch a Sunbeam ...	15
Trial of Sir Jasper	25
Two Boys and Raven's Nest ...	8
Two Housebreakers	12
Two Months in India with a Camera	40

U, V

Umbrella, O'Toole Adventures ..	9
Unskilful Ratcatchers	12
Underground Life	90
Venice	30
Vulgar Boy	6
Voyage of the "Challenger" ..	42

W, X, Y, Z

Wales, North	50
Wanderings in Paris	50
Washington City	50
,, to Yellowstone Park	50
Weather Prospects	6
Wedding Bells	10
Westminster Abbey	36
Whisky Demon	12
Whittington and his Cat	24
Witches' Frolic	12
Woodman, The Little	12
World Inverted	6
Worship of Bacchus	14
Wreaths and Mottoes	36
Wye River	45
Yacht, Round the World in a ...	45
Zoological Gardens, The Animals	215
,, ,, H.R.H. The Prince of Wales's Animals ...	18

PRICE OF

THE FOREGOING LANTERN PHOTOGRAPHS.

PLAIN 12/-

COLOURED 18/6

TRADE DISCOUNT LIST ON APPLICATION.

SIX PENCE.

Third Edition Revised and Enlarged.
24th Thousand.

BEGINNER'S GUIDE
TO
PHOTOGRAPHY.

Copyright.

[FOR PRESS OPINIONS SEE OVER.

PRESS OPINIONS.

Third Edition. Beginner's Guide to Photography, **6d.**

GRAPHIC.

"The 'Beginner's Guide to Photography' (Perken, Son and Rayment), by a 'Fellow of the Chemical Society,' is a useful little manual for amateur photographers. It contains brief and concise directions for taking, developing, and printing the negative, while there is a valuable article on that bugbear of all amateurs—'Exposure,' by Mr. A. S Platts, containing some exceedingly useful exposure tables "

DAILY NEWS.

"Under the title of the 'Beginner's Guide to Photography,' by a 'Fellow of the Chemical Society,' Perken, Son and Rayment have published a useful handbook for all interested in the art of photography. An article on 'Exposure,' and some carefully compiled exposure tables, by Mr. A. S. Platts, must be of value to all amateurs."

St. STEPHEN'S REVIEW.

"'Beginner's Guide to Photography,' published by Perken, Son and Rayment, 99, Hatton Garden, London.—The fashionable art science, Photography, is most explicitly set forth without the confusing technicalities employed in most works on this subject. The difficult matter of 'Choice of Apparatus' has a chapter devoted to it, in which the special advantages of each kind of camera and lens is detailed. Altogether this book may be said to be of the greatest value to all who practise photography."

ILLUSTRATED SPORTING & DRAMATIC.

"The 'Beginner's Guide to Photography.'—With this title a six penny book has been published by Messrs. Perken, Son and Rayment, of 99, Hatton Garden, which we find both simple and practical. By following its instructions carefully the amateur will save much disappointment in the sense of blurred pictures, and much expense for spoilt plates."

MORNING POST.

"The 'Beginner's Guide to Photography' is one of the best works on this popular and fascinating art yet published. The author thoroughly understands his subject. Messrs. Perken, Son and Rayment, Hatton Garden, are the publishers."

WHITEHALL REVIEW.

"'Beginner's Guide to Photography.' (Perken, Son and Rayment.)—This is an excellent treatise which all amateurs who have taken up photography as an amusement should peruse."

ARMY & NAVY GAZETTE,

"Messrs. Perken, Son and Rayment send us the second edition of their 'Beginner's Guide to Photography,' a plain and practical handbook as to how to buy and use a camera, with many particulars concerning lenses and other matters, for which the publishers are celebrated as makers."

COURT JOURNAL.

"Messrs. Perken, Son and Rayment, one of the largest and most popular makers of photographic apparatus, publish a most useful little work entitled, 'Beginner's Guide to Photography,' in which the several operations of taking, developing and printing the photograph are described with great clearness, and in a manner most suitable to those who are handling a camera for the first time. While those who have not yet provided themselves with the necessary apparatus cannot do better than peruse the valuable chapter on 'The Choice of Apparatus,' and patronise this firm for their purchases."

JEWELLER & METALWORKER.

"'Beginner's Guide,' published by Messrs. Perken, Son and Rayment, of 99, Hatton Garden, at the small sum of six pence. It is a work which can be relied upon, and the language of it is easy of comprehension, a great merit in works of this description."

ILLUSTRATED LONDON NEWS.

"The 'Beginner's Guide to Photography,' published by Messrs. Perken, Son and Rayment, of Hatton Garden, treats clearly and concisely of the apparatus and requirements necessary to engage in the delightful pastime of photography, and will be found most useful to amateurs."

LADY'S PICTORIAL.

"'Beginner's Guide to Photography.' (Perken, Son and Rayment, 'Optimus.') Revised and enlarged edition, 6d. It is clear and explicit, quite free from unnecessary and confusing technicalities. I can safely recommend this little work to any of our readers who contemplate taking up photography."

ENGLISH MECHANIC.

"'Beginner's Guide to Photography.' Messrs. Perken, Son and Rayment, of Hatton Garden, have issued a second edition of this useful little work, which has already reached a very large sale."

THE
MAGIC LANTERN:

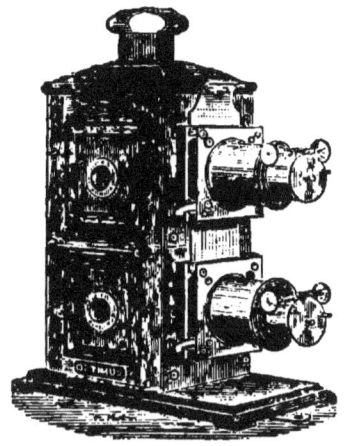

ITS
CONSTRUCTION AND USE.

Copyright.

PUBLISHED BY
PERKEN, SON, & RAYMENT,
99, HATTON GARDEN, E.C.

[FOR PRESS OPINIONS SEE OVER.

PRESS OPINIONS.—" *The Magic Lantern: Its Construction and Use.*"

ILLUSTRATED LONDON NEWS, January 4th, 1890.

"For the entertainment of young folk at Christmas holiday evening parties, the magic-lantern is the most powerful instrument, which has been vastly improved by modern science and skill. An instructive little sixpenny book, written by a Fellow of the Chemical Society, the author of '*The Beginner's Guide to Photography*,' is published by Messrs. Perken, Son, and Rayment, of Hatton Garden. It explains, clearly and precisely, the construction and use of this ingenious optical apparatus, and the advantages of the new and improved magic lanterns, which ought not to be ignorantly or carelessly handled. They seem to be as superior to those which were familiar to the childhood of people now rather elderly, as is the naval artillery of the present day to the ship-guns of Trafalgar."

ILL. SPORTING & DRAMATIC NEWS. January 11th, 1890.

"*The Magic Lantern its Construction and Use.* By a Fellow of the Chemical Society.—Messrs. Perken, Son, and Rayment, of 99, Hatton Garden, publish at sixpence, a little volume, uniform with their treatises on photography and electricity, which deals very lucidly with the subject of the magic lantern. The principles which regulate the construction of magic lanterns, simple and complex, and the methods of illumination, including the preparation of the limelight, are detailed in a way to enable anyone with the most moderate aptitude for scientific matters to master the subject without difficulty."

MORNING POST, January 18th, 1890.

"Messrs. Perken, Son, and Rayment publish a little manual on '*The Magic Lantern, its Construction and Use.*' It explains the numerous improvements which have recently been made in this popular optical instrument, as well as the operator's duties while exhibiting the pictures. Many other matters connected with the use of the lantern, whether for pleasure or educational purposes, are included."

ENGLISH MECHANIC, January 1st, 1890.

"'*The Magic Lantern.*'—Messrs Perken, Son, and Rayment have issued a cheap and useful manual of the magic lantern, explaining the principle of its construction, describing the various forms, and giving directions for its use. All who wish to have a lantern and learn how to manipulate it will find the information required in this handy book."

ARMY & NAVY GAZETTE, January 11th, 1890.

"At this season of the year many amateurs are in search of hints as to how to manage their magic-lanterns. They cannot do better than read an admirable *brochure*, *The Magic Lantern, its Construction and Use.* which Messrs. Perken, Son, and Rayment, of Hatton Garden, have just published. Its instructions are exceedingly simple, lucid, and direct. No amateur following them need hesitate to make use of the oxy-hydrogen or other similar light, and can scarcely fail to succeed with his Lantern.'

AMATEUR PHOTOGRAPHER. January 17th, 1890.

"*The Magic Lantern, its Construction and Use,*" is the name of a convenient little hand-book published by Messrs. Perken, Son, and Rayment. It deals with the subject of single lanterns with oil lamps, of the limelight and method of making oxygen, of bi-unial and tri-unial lanterns, and the making and colouring of slides. It also deals with the application of the spectroscope to the lantern, and with the aphengescope. A beginner will find it a valuable help."

BRITISH JOURNAL OF PHOTOGRAPHY, January 10th, 1890.

"RECEIVED.—"*The Magic Lantern: its Construction and Use,*" published by Perken, Son and Rayment. A handy manual, a useful feature in which is a price l ca alogue of the numerous lanterns and fittings connected therewith sold by the publishers."

THE SPORTING LIFE, December, 28th, 1889.

"'*The Magic Lantern, its Construction and Use,*' is the title of a clever little manual published by Messrs. Perken, Son, and Rayment, 99, Hatton Garden. A perusal of the sound and practical advice contained in its columns should enable one to "build" a lantern of his own, the "tip" being obtainable at the small cost of six pennies."

"FIGARO," January 4th, 1890.

'At this season of the year a little volume called '*The Magic Lantern, its Construction and Use,*' published by Perken, Son, and Rayment, 99, Hatton Garden, will be found extremely useful. It contains a great deal of technical information, and is abundantly illustrated. I do not quite see how anyone who is starting 'the most popular of optical instruments' can do without it. Some excellent hints are given at the close as to the tools which it is necessary for the owner of a lantern to possess."

ONE SHILLING.

INTENSITY COILS
HOW MADE & HOW USED
BY "DYER"

SOLD BY ALL OPTICIANS.

[FOR PRESS OPINIONS SEE OVER.

PRESS OPINIONS.—"*Intensity Coils: How Made and How Used.*"

ENGLISH MECHANIC.

"In the preface it warns us that it is not put forth as a scientific exposition of e matter; yet, for all that, many of the explanations are clear and good, and rections for experiments easily to be followed."

ELECTRICAL ENGINEER.

"'Intensity Coils: How Made and How Used.' By Dyer. Sixteenth Edition. London: Perken, Son and Rayment. A book that has reached a sixteenth edition, and which has been before the world for many years, must contain information that is wanted. The Ruhmkorff coil has become one of the most interesting pieces of apparatus in electrical engineering in its comparatively recent development, known as the transformer. This book shows very clearly the historical views held about the coil, and from the amateur constructor's point of view is most valuable, in that it explains clearly how to make and how to use a coil. A great many lecture experiments are described."

CHEMIST AND DRUGGIST.

"'Intensity Coils.' By 'Dyer.' London: Perken Son and Rayment, 99, Hatton Garden. 1s. This is one of those valuable little popular manuals which convey a sound elementary knowledge of an important subject in a concise manner. It describes the principal batteries, deals fully with making coils, and illustrates their use by numerous experiments. There are in addition brief explanations of the electric light, the telegraph, telephone, phonegraph, &c."

ARCHITECT

"'Intensity Coils.' This is the title of one of the publications of Messrs. Perken, Son and Rayment, of Hatton Garden. It is a "beginner's guide to electricity," describing the way to make batteries, bells. coils, electric light, telegraphs, phonographs, telephones, &c. It is already passing through its sixteenth edition, or the 128th thousand. One of the merits of this brochure is that it does not require an expert to understand it."

PHOTOGRAPHIC NEWS.

"Messrs Perken, Son and Rayment, the sixteenth edition of 'Intensity Coils, being a beginner's guide to electricity, describing the way to make batteries, bells, coils, electric light, telegraphs, phonographs, and so on."

PHOTOGRAPHY.

"'Intensity Coils.' Perken, Son and Rayment, 99, Hatton Garden, E.C. This forms one of the firm's well-known publications, and is a sort of beginner's guide to electricity, describing the way to make batteries, coils, lights, bells, telegraphs, telephones, phonographs, &c."

CHEMICAL NEWS.

"The induction coil has now come into such general favour, and is used for such varied purposes as a medical instrument, a means of scientific research, and an amusing toy for winter's evenings, that several treatises have lately appeared, describing the best methods of its manufacture and management. The object of the little work before us is explained in the following manner in the preface:—

"What is an intensity coil? How does it differ from other coils? How is it made? What will it do? These and similar questions are being continually asked, and to furnish intelligible replies to them the following pages have been written It is not a scientific treatise that is here offered to the public, but simply the necessary instructions that those who want to make or use intensity coils desire to obtain."

CITY PRESS.

"'Intensity Coils.' By 'Dyer' (Perken, Son and Rayment). When a handbook, as for instance the one now demanding attention, retains its position for nearly a quarter of a century, few will be inclined to dispute the contention that it is a work possessing considerably more backbone than the generality of such publications. The present book was first published in the year 1867, and it is now in its 16th edition. In its pages will be found, given in an eminently readable form, much that will serve to instruct the young idea concerning the electric light, the telephone, the microphone, and other wonders which, more or less, are associated with the great American inventor, Edison. With all the confidence we displayed when twenty years ago we noticed the first edition, we can heartily commend this handbook to the notice of our readers as a publication 'which will be of service to all persons' engaged in the interesting experiments about which 'Dyer' has so much to say."

THE OLDEST PHOTOGRAPHIC JOURNAL.

Estab. 1854.   PUBLISHED EVERY FRIDAY.   Price Twopence.

The British Journal of Photography

THE BRITISH JOURNAL OF PHOTOGRAPHY is the Representative of all the leading British and Foreign Photographic Societies, and is pre-eminently the recognised medium of the **Professional and Amateur.** Its pages contain the very latest news connected with the Art-Science.

THE BRITISH JOURNAL OF PHOTOGRAPHY is extensively circulated, not only in Great Britain and Ireland, but throughout the world, and is a most valuable medium for Photographic Advertisements, ensuring them the largest amount of publicity.

THE BRITISH JOURNAL OF PHOTOGRAPHY AS A MEDIUM of direct and certain communication with all classes of Amateur and Professional Photographers throughout the world, strongly commends itself to Photographic Advertisers.

THE BRITISH JOURNAL OF PHOTOGRAPHY.—All LARGE ADVERTISEMENTS should reach the publishing offices not later than TUESDAYS, but SMALL ADVERTISEMENTS can be received up to 6 p.m. on WEDNESDAYS.

SCALE OF CHARGES FOR ADVERTISEMENTS.

	£ s. d.		£ s. d.
WHOLE PAGE 1 Insertion	... 4 10 0	QUARTER PAGE 1 Insertion...	1 7 6
HALF PAGE ,,	... 2 10 0	FIFTH PAGE ,,	... 1 2 6
THIRD PAGE .,	... 1 15 0	SIXTH PAGE ,,	... 0 19 0
EIGHTH PAGE ...	1 Insertion ... £0 15 0.		

REDUCTION FOR A SERIES OF INSERTIONS.

CHARGE FOR SPECIAL INSET CIRCULAR, ON ANY COLOUR PAPER: One page, £5 5s.; Two Pages, £8 10s.; Four pages £12 12s. Advertisements on the Cover, and a few others of great prominence, are charged by Special Agreement.

.* BLOCKS AND CONFORM COPY of Advertisements are received subject to approval of Publishers.

SINGLE COLUMN TRADE ADVERTISEMENTS.

	Once	6 Inserts.	13 Inserts.	26 Inserts.	52 Inserts.
Half Inch	£0 3 0	£0 3 0	£0 3 0	£0 3 0	£0 3 0
Three-quarter Inch ...	0 4 6	0 4 0	0 3 6	0 3 0	0 3 0
One Inch	0 6 0	0 5 6	0 4 6	0 4 0	0 3 0

SINGLE COLUMN TRADE ADVERTISEMENTS (PREPAID).

	Once	6 Inserts.	13 Inserts.	26 Inserts.	52 Inserts.
Half Inch	£0 2 0	£0 2 0	£0 2 0	£0 2 0	£0 2 0
Three-quarter Inch ...	0 3 0	0 3 0	0 3 0	0 3 0	0 2 6
One Inch	0 4 0	0 4 0	0 4 0	0 3 6	0 3 0

Charge for small Prepaid Advertisements of Four Lines (each Line containing Seven Words) of the following Classes ONLY:

Professional Photographers Requiring Assistants ... ...
Operators, &c., Wanting Situations ... ... } 1/-
Photographic Premises to be Let or Sold ... ... } Prepaid
Second-hand Photographic Apparatus for Sale... ... ... } Rate.
Each Additional Line (Seven Words), Sixpence.

₊ Communications relating to Advertisements and general business affairs should be addressed to HENRY GREENWOOD & Co., 2, York Street, Covent Garden, London.

SUBSCRIPTION POST FREE.
(UNITED KINGDOM AND THE CHANNEL ISLES),

One Year, **10/10**. Half Year, **5/5**.   Quarter Year, **2/9**.

France, Belgium, United States, Canada, Australia, New Zealand, Africa (North and West Coasts), Newfoundland, Germany, Portugal, Spain, Italy, Egypt, and Argentine Republic, 13s.; ; India, China, Japan, Africa (East Coast), &c., 15s. 2d.

London: HENRY GREENWOOD & CO, PUBLISHERS,
2, YORK STREET, COVENT GARDEN.

PHOTOGRAPHIC PUBLICATIONS

THE PHOTOGRAPHIC NEWS, a Weekly Record of the Progress of Photography. Published every Friday, price 2d.

INSTRUCTION IN PHOTOGRAPHY. Capt. ABNEY, C.B., R.E., F.R.S. Eighth Edition corrected to date, considerably enlarged, and profusely illustrated. Price 3s. 6d., per post, 3s. 10d. "The standard manual of the English photographic practitioner."

PHOTOGRAPHIC PRIMERS. By same Author. No. 1.—NEGATIVE MAKING. Price 1s., per post, 1s. 1½d.

THE ART AND PRACTICE OF SILVER PRINTING. By H. P. ROBINSON & CAPT. ABNEY, C.B., R.E., F.R.S. Price 2s. 6d., per post, 2s. 8d.

RECENT ADVANCES IN PHOTOGRAPHY. Being the Cantor Lectures for 1882. By Capt. ABNEY, R.E., F.R.S. Reprinted with additional matter, from the *Journal of the Society of Arts.* Price 6d., per post 6½d.

BURTON'S MODERN PHOTOGRAPHY. Comprising Practical Instructions in Working Gelatine Dry Plates. By Prof. W. K. BURTON, C.E. Seventh Edition, very considerably enlarged. Price 1s. per post, 1s. 2d.

OPTICS FOR PHOTOGRAPHERS. By Prof. W. K. BURTON, C.E., Author of "Burton's Modern Photography," "Burton's Note-Book for Photographers," &c., &c. Price 1s., per post 1s. 2d.

BURTON'S POCKET BOOK FOR PHOTOGRAPHERS: Including the usual space for Notes, &c., with Tables for Facilitating Exposures. Price, paper covers, 9d., per post 10d.; cloth, 1s., per post 1s. 1d.

A CASKET OF PHOTOGRAPHIC GEMS. A Collection of 500 Dodges, Receipts, Entertaining Experiments. &c., in connection with the Art of Photography and its branches. Collected, classified, and arranged for ready reference, by W. INGLES ROGERS. Price 1s., per post 1s. 2d.

THE ART OF PHOTOGRAPHIC PAINTING. By A. H. BOOL, Price 1s., per post 1s. 1d.

THE HANDBOOK OF PHOTOGRAPHIC TERMS. An Alphabetical arrangement of the Processes, Formulæ, Applications, &c., of Photography for Ready Reference. Compiled by WILLIAM HEIGHWAY. Price 2s. 6d. per post, 2s. 8d.

PRACTICAL PORTRAIT PHOTOGRAPHY. A Handbook for the Dark Room, the Skylight, and the Printing Room. By the Same Author. Price 1s., per post 1s. 1½d.

PHOTOGRAPHIC PRINTER'S ASSISTANT. By the same Author Price 1s., per post 1s. 1d.

ESTHETICS OF PHOTOGRAPHY. By the same Author. Being Hints on Posing and Lighting the Sitter. Price 1s. per post, 1s. 1½d.

ELEMENTARY LESSONS ON SILVER PRINTING. By W. M. ASHMAN. Revised and reprinted from the *Photographic News*, with additions to date. Price 1s. 6d., per post 1s. 8d.

ENAMELLING AND RETOUCHING. A Practical Photographic Treatise. By P. PIQUEPE. Price 2s. 6d., per post 2s. 8d.

PHOTO-MICROGRAPHY; Or, How to Photograph Microscopic Objects. By I. H. JENNINGS. Also, A CHAPTER ON PREPARING BACTERIA. By Dr. R. L. MADDOX. Price 3s., per post 3s. 2d.

THE SPECTROSCOPE AND ITS RELATION TO PHOTOGRAPHY. By C. RAY WOODS. Price 6d., per post 7d.

PIPER & CARTER,

Printers, Publishers, & Advertising Agents,

5, FURNIVAL STREET, HOLBORN, E.C.

THE OLDEST WEEKLY PHOTOGRAPHIC PAPER.

THE
PHOTOGRAPHIC NEWS

Edited by T. C. HEPWORTH, F.C.S.

A Weekly Record of the Progress of Photography.

THE PHOTOGRAPHIC NEWS

Has long been recognised as the guide and instructor of the beginner, the medium of communication and interchange of ideas between more advanced students, and the record of all improvements and discoveries which take place in Photography and the allied sciences.

PUBLISHED EVERY FRIDAY, PRICE 2d.

ALL WHO HAVE LANTERNS SHOULD READ

THE

Book ══ 3/6

OF THE

3/6 Lantern

By T. C. HEPWORTH.

It is the standard work on the subject, and contains full and precise directions for making and colouring lantern pictures.

HAZELL, WATSON & VINEY, 1, CREED LANE, E.C.

☞ **The largest circulation of any Photographic Paper in the World.**

PHOTOGRAPHY:

The Journal of the Amateur, the Profession, and the Trade.

EVERY THURSDAY.   ONE PENNY.

Editorial Contributors:
CAPT. W. DE W. ABNEY, C.B., F.R.S.; PROF. W. K. BURTON C.E.; GEORGE DAVISON; CHAPMAN JONES; ANDREW PRINGLE; FRANK M. SUTCLIFFE.
EDITOR—HENRY STURMEY. SUB-EDITOR—W. D. WELFORD.

The special features are:—Scientific and Technical Articles by well-known writers—The Question Box, in which questions on all subjects are asked and answered by readers of the paper, with a series of prizes for the senders of replies—Prize Competitions—Snap Shots—Items of Interest—Interviews with Prominent Members of the Trade; and the price—One Penny.

A SPECIMEN COPY WILL BE SENT GRATIS AND POST FREE.

What they Think of It:—

" *Photography* is a positive success."—*Wilson's Photographic Magazine.*
" A stirring, newsy journal."—*St. Louis Photographer.*
" It is very interesting, and far ahead of the other photographic papers."—GERALD STONEY, Gateshead.
" I look upon *Photography* now as part of my weekly diet, as it suits my constitution."—MOORE, Dartford.
" When I have read the pages of one week's issue I am anxious to see the next."—F. LEWIS, Derby.
" Your journal, like the 'Pickwick' pen 'comes as a boon and a blessing to men.'"—J. C. CHRISTIE, Old Cathcart.
" You may be sure I shall prize this my *first* silver medal, and I shall not want to look at it to remind me of *Photography*, as I always have this paper for dessert on Thursdays."—J. W. EVANS, Wolverhampton.
" I think your paper a marvel of cheapness. I had great difficulty in getting it regularly, or even at all, at first, but since I have succeeded I think all my early trouble has been liberally repaid."—A. C. ANDERSON, Arbroath.

London: ILIFFE & SON, 3, ST. BRIDE ST., E.C.
AND ALL BOOKSELLERS AND BOOKSTALLS.

Editorial and Advertisement Offices:
19, HERTFORD STREET, COVENTRY.

ILIFFE AND SON'S PHOTOGRAPHIC PUBLICATIONS.

PHOTOGRAPHY. Edited by Henry Sturmey. The only penny Photographic Paper in the World. Every Thursday. Price 1d.; post free, 1½d.

"PHOTOGRAPHY" Annual for 1891. Edited by Henry Sturmey. A compendium of information and statistics of the year. Demy 8vo.; 300 pages. Price 2s.; post free 2s. 6d.

PHOTOGRAPHY FOR ALL. An Elementary Text Book and Introduction to the Art of Taking Photographs. By W. Jerome Harrison, F.G.S., European Editor of "The International Annual of Anthony's Bulletin." Sewed, 1s.; post free, 1s. 2d.

THE INTERNATIONAL ANNUAL of Anthony's Photographic Bulletin. Vol. III. 1890-91. Edited by W. Jerome Harrison, F.G.S. and A. H. Elliott, Ph.D. Containing nine page illustrations, and 500 pages of reading matter. Price 2s.; post free, 2s. 4½d.

PRACTICAL PHOTO-MICROGRAPHY by the latest methods. By Andrew Pringle, F.R.M.S. Six full-page plates. Price 10s. 6d.; post free, 11s.

COLLOTYPE & PHOTO-LITHOGRAPHY. By Dr. Julius Schnauss. Translated, with the sanction and assistance of the author, by E. C. Middleton. Together with all the original illustrations, and an Appendix on Steam Presses. Price 5s.; post free, 5s. 4½d.

THE PROCESSES OF PURE PHOTOGRAPHY. By W. K. Burton, C.E., and Andrew Pringle. A standard work; freely illustrated. Price 4s. 6d.; post free, 4s. 10½d.

THE PHOTOGRAPHER'S INDISPENSABLE HANDBOOK. A Complete Cyclopædia on the subject of Photographic Apparatus, Material and Processes. Complied by Walter D. Welford; Edited by Henry Sturmey. Price 2s. 6d.; post free, 2s. 10½d.

THE INDISPENSABLE HANDBOOK TO THE OPTICAL LANTERN. A complete Cyclopædia on the subject of Optical Lanterns, Slides, and Accessory Apparatus. Compiled by Walter D. Welford; Edited by Henry Sturmey. Price 2s. 6d; post free 2s. 10½d.

AN INTRODUCTION TO THE SCIENCE AND PRACTICE OF PHOTOGRAPHY. By Chapman Jones, F.I.C., F.C.S., Demonstrator of Practical-Chemistry in the Normal School of Science and Royal School of Mines. Sewed, 2s. 6d.; cloth 3s. 6d. Postage, 4½d.

THE ART AND PRACTICE OF INTERIOR PHOTOGRAPHY. By F. W. Mills, Member of the Camera Club, and of the Huddersfield Photographic Society. Demy 8vo., cloth. Illustrated. Price 2s. 6d.; post free, 2s. 9d.

PHOTOGRAPHY FOR ARCHITECTS. By F. W. Mills, author of "The Art and Practice of Interior Photography." Demy 8vo., cloth, illustrated. Price 2s. 6d.; post free, 2s. 9d.

PHOTOGRAVURE. By W. T. Wilkinson. A complete Text Book on the Subject; with illustrations. Price 1s. 6d.; post free 1s. 7d.

PHOTOGRAPHY IN A NUTSHALL. By the "Kernel." Crown 8vo. Price 1s.; Post free 1s. 2d.; Cloth Bound and Interleaved 2s. 6d.; post free 2s. 9d.

MATERIA PHOTOGRAPHICA. By C. J. Leaper, F.C.S. A treatise on the manufacture, uses and properties of the substances employed in Photography. Crown 8vo., cloth, 250 pages, largely illustrated. Price 5s.; post free 5s. 3d.
[In the Press.

MILITARY PHOTOGRAPHY. By O. E. Wheeler, late Captain 1st. Leicestershire Regiment. *[In Preparation.*

PHOTOGRAPHIC PASTIMES. By Hermann Schnauss. Translated from the second German Edition, with numerous illustrations. Crown 8vo.; stiff covers. Price 1s.; Post free 1s. 1½d. *[In Preparation.*

LONDON:
ILIFFE AND SON, 3, ST. BRIDE ST., LONDON, E.C.

THE CAMERA.

A Monthly Magazine for all those interested in the Practice of Photography.

Published on the first of every Month.

PRICE THREEPENCE.

Annual Subscription, including home postage, Four Shillings.

THE CAMERA is the Oldest and Best Monthly Magazine devoted to the Art of Photography, and has the Largest Genuine Circulation amongst high-class readers both at home and abroad.

THE CAMERA contains original articles by well-known writers, of practical interest to all Amateur and Professional Photographers.

THE CAMERA is profusely illustrated. Vol. v. containing twelve monthly parts is now ready, and can be had of the Publishers, Price 5s., post-free 5s. 6d.

THE PHOTOGRAPHER'S
DIARY & DESK-BOOK for 1891.

Comprising a Diary, Three Days on a Page, interleaved with Blotting Paper, and a mass of useful information peculiarly interesting to Photographers, including reliable Formulæ, printed in such large type that they can be read distinctly in the dim light of the Photographic dark room.

Price 1s. 6d., Post-free 2s.

Liberal discount to the Trade and members of Photographic Clubs.

55 & 56, CHANCERY LANE,
LONDON, W.C.

PATENTS OBTAINED.
DESIGNS AND TRADE MARKS REGISTERED
IN ALL COUNTRIES.

TONGUE & BIRKBECK,
Patent Agents,
34, SOUTHAMPTON BUILDINGS,
CHANCERY LANE, LONDON, W.C.

Opposite the Government Patent Office.

ESTABLISHED 1859.

British and Foreign Patents obtained.

Opinions and Advice given on all matters relating to Patents or Inventions.

Searches made to ascertain novelty of Inventions.

Large experience and practice in connection with Photographic Patents and infringements thereof.

No charge made for Correspondence.

www.ingramcontent.com/pod-product-compliance
Lightning Source LLC
Chambersburg PA
CBHW031443160426
43195CB00010BB/829